D1236891

DATE DUE

STARTING OUT

A Mid-life Journey into Wild Land

IN THE AFTERNOON

JILL FRAYNE

RANDOM HOUSE CANADA

COPYRIGHT © 2002 JILL FRAYNE

All rights reserved under International and Pan-American
Copyright Conventions. No part of this book may be reproduced
in any form or by any electronic or mechanical means, including information
storage and retrieval systems, without permission in writing from the
publisher, except by a reviewer, who may quote brief passages in a review.
Published in 2002 by Random House Canada, a division of Random House
of Canada Limited. Distributed by Random House of Canada Limited.

Random House Canada and colophon are trademarks.

National Library of Canada Cataloguing in Publication Data

Frayne, Jill
Starting out in the afternoon : a mid-life journey into wild land

ISBN 0-679-31119-X

1. Frayne, Jill—Journeys—Canada.   2. Middle age—
Psychological aspects.   3. Canada—Description and travel.
I. Title.

FC27.F726A3 2002   917.104'648   C2001-903486-5
CT310.F65A3 2002

www.randomhouse.ca

Text design: CS Richardson

Printed and bound in the United States of America

10 9 8 7 6 5 4 3 2 1

To Marni, my old canoeing pal

CONTENTS

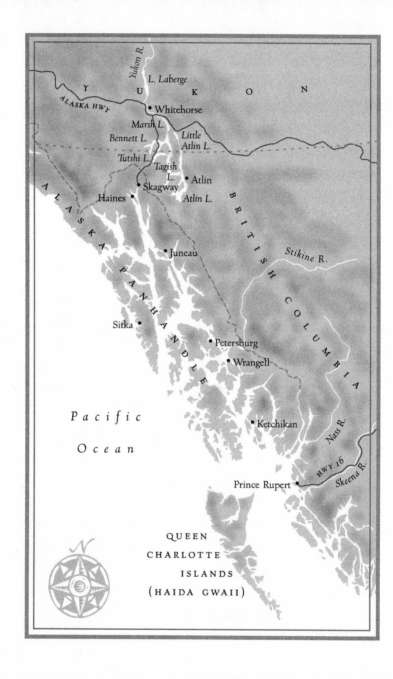

One

STARTING OUT

*T*he spring my daughter finished high school, I packed up the car with everything I'd need to live outdoors for three months, everything I could think of for travel by car, kayak, bicycle and ferry, glanced one more time around my yard, which would go unplanted that year, and backed out of the driveway.

My first night I got as far as Georgian Bay, turning in at a provincial park—empty this early in the season—and setting up camp beside a bog with a huge dome of granite in the middle. I was too miserable to eat, the prospect of the journey closing my throat. I sat cross-legged in my tent, a nylon clam open to the white twilight, relieved to be out of the car, with its summers' worth of paraphernalia: camping gear and groceries, feather pillows and books, backpack and rainwear. We stress ourselves in order to change, and this time I'd chosen solitude and wild land as the forge.

After three days of driving I was still in Ontario. We think of the province as a pan of paved-over ground along the shore of Lake Ontario, a stretch of a hundred kilometres where most of us live, but the real Ontario is the Precambrian Shield—the great wastes of rock overarching tiny southern Ontario in an endless tract of elemental granite and pointed black spruce. The land up here is ponderous, orchestral, especially where the road follows Lake Superior, giving tremendous views of the hills standing up to their mighty shoulders in the sea. Once you leave Superior, though, and plunge into boreal forest—the dark, acid, interminable land west of Thunder Bay—the project of getting out of Ontario becomes daunting. This rock carapace is nothing less than the bulge of the earth's raw core, scarred, disordered, primordial. The density and weight of the rock have an emotional quality that penetrates the mind. Time seems to clog in the runty trees and gravity tugs in a bold, unbounded way like nowhere else.

When the prairie comes at last, it's like emerging from a spelunking expedition, rescued by the sky, hauled up and out into the light. On the prairie there is no rock at all, no jagged angles, no glittering lakes, no lowering skies stabbed with evergreens. The morphology of prairie is round.

Past Kenora, the heavy sky and cut rock of the Shield quickly give way to open Manitoba prairie, the road straightening and stretching till it looks like a drawn wire slicing into the horizon.

I ducked south of Winnipeg and drove into the setting sun, the evening sky a violet shawl around me.

West of Winnipeg the horizon was dead flat, the only feature the occasional picket of willows barricading a farm. Secondary roads ran along beside the highway with pinprick vehicles, miles off, raising plumes of dust. Farmers, still on their machines in the spring twilight, turned the black ground. Bugs loaded up and baked on the car grille, and any time I slowed, the cool fields filled with birdsong. I turned off the highway and, in the last mauve light of day, found a campground on Lake Winnipeg in a willow grove full of singing birds and shadflies.

THOSE FIRST DAYS, driving queasily through the Precambrian scenery, unreeling the tender thread between me and home, I had doubts about my expedition, alone in a car on a three-month excursion to the Yukon.

We all have spells of high suggestibility, and I was in one the previous September when I heard a radio interview with a painter, Doris McCarthy. She would have been close to eighty at the time, her voice cheerful and nicotine-cracked, her breathtaking Arctic canvases floating in my memory. At nine-thirty in the morning, while I drove to work from my home near Uxbridge, she and Peter Gzowski were reminiscing about Pangnirtung, a village on Baffin Island they both know. One of them recalled being there in July and, from a window, watching the freed ice move up the bay on the tide and out again on the ebb. Eyeing the approaching Scarborough skyline from my car, a fortress of upended concrete shoe-boxes under a bloom of smog, I was gripped by this image, by the elegance of this event, and I set my mind to go there.

Ideas that lay hold like this have to turn immutable in the mind if they're going to amount to anything. When I discovered that Pangnirtung is not reachable by car, I could not let myself be deterred. I gave notice at my job and started telling people I was going to drive up to the Arctic the coming summer.

It was not so whimsical a resolve as it may seem. I'd managed a show of equanimity through my daughter's adolescence and through a long renegotiation of terms with the man I'd been living with. I'd been seven years at a counselling agency fifty miles from home, where I spent my time listening to other harried families. I was watching for a harbinger of change. I believe in the accuracy of ideas that come in this way. After long suspense, long inertia, everything rushes together at once in a notion that has great force. This northern image had such vitality that I would go north even if I couldn't get to the ice floes.

JUNE 17, 1990

The shrubs around the picnic table where I sit writing this morning are shaking with birds. I see kinds I thought had vanished—

those darting ones that never seem to land—and a Baltimore ori-
ole, his breast the colour of marigolds. Walking in the fields the
other side of the thicket this morning, I saw a wedge of pelicans
pass overhead, shining white birds rowing the sky without making a sound. They flew exactly in sync, their huge wings closing
the air in slow unison. Beat . . . beat . . . beat . . . glide.

I pack up finally, whisking shadflies off my tent fly, and retrace
the route out to the highway. In spite of the heat it's barely spring,
last year's fields still white and razed. Only the rims of ditches show
a rind of green. The houses, in clouds of muzzy willow, are built
tall with narrow, tree-blocked windows, and have a secretive, fore-
stalling look. Pickup trucks tilt in the front yards as though the
drivers had to get out fast. I conjure secret strife going on behind
the walls in rooms of filtered light. There's a dogged atmosphere to
these places, as if people living here are pitched against an enemy.

As the landscape empties, road signs get more frequent as though
to keep up contact with motorists as we drive beyond the pale.

CHECK YOUR ODOMETER.

START CHECK NOW. 0——1——2——

PUT YOUR GARBAGE INTO ORBIT. 5 KMS.

ORBIT. 10 SECS.

I BEGIN TO look forward to Saskatchewan, which can't afford road
commentary and garbage cans resembling spaceships.

OVER THE WINTER, while the ice in the yard turned crusty and slowly melted, I put together a plan. I wanted to go north but west as well, to the rain forests and the Pacific Ocean. Someone at the yoga centre where I took classes a couple of times a week told me about Ecosummer, a touring company, environmentally friendly, that takes people to remote places they'd never get to on their own. South Moresby, in the Queen Charlotte Islands, had been in the news because of controversy over logging in Lyle Island. I looked at the region on a map, a fang of islands on the edge of the continental shelf halfway up the coast of British Columbia. I got Ecosummer's brochure and spotted a fifteen-day trip in kayaks to the old Haida hunt camps and villages in South Moresby. The idea of thousand-year-old cedar groves on Lyle Island set me dreaming. I'd never been in a kayak or any small craft on the open sea, but the timing of this trip made it possible. I could be in Prince Rupert by the end of June, a ferry ride from the Charlottes. I could drive my car to the coast in time for the kayak expedition, and from Prince Rupert, when the trip was over, take the ferry north to the Yukon.

TEN MONTHS after the radio broadcast, on a day in June, I was ready to go, my ten-year-old Mazda sagging with gear, a mongrel bicycle strapped to the roof.

I started my adventure by backtracking south. My daughter, Bree, needed a lift to Toronto. When we got to the big residential neighbourhood at the top of the city, she stood solemnly in the street under the spring trees and bade me goodbye. She'd write her final exams while I was away. I'd miss her high school graduation. Alone in the car leaving town, sunk in misgivings, I ran over a sparrow and, like a starter's gun, this dismal popping sound began my trip.

BY NOW I have my travel legs. Somewhere out here thoughts of home begin to peter out and I stop keeping time with life back there. The queasiness has passed and I feel frisky, which I attribute to the out-and-out kindness of prairie. It lulls me, the roundness of every shape, every bush and stream clinging to the ground, bending and winding under the wind, the whole earth suppliant to the sky.

Out here I've bedded down with the land, lock, stock and barrel. I thought I'd stop in restaurants to get a break and talk to people, but I don't want to go indoors. A couple of times I've pulled off into some place and after the waitress brings the water, I get up and wander out, climb into the car and drive away. Down the road I pull over and make a sandwich on the hood.

I thought I'd eat well. I brought my soup enhancers, camp stove and fast-cooking grains, but on the buggy Shield the coziest thing was to crawl into the back seat with my sleeping bag and open a can of baked beans. It's such a liberty to be in my own company, queen of all my choices. Heaps of freedom, which is the allure of travelling alone in a car, makes me giddy. I whisk along, nestled in the car, avoiding buildings, eyes guzzling the passing landscape.

Solitude is not what I thought, though. I expected to fall in upon myself, oblivious to the world, strike up an interior life looping back upon itself, a plane of thought sealed off from experience, like convalescence or retreat. But travelling alone through landscape is not that. It's more like a relationship—not with a human, not as though one had company, but as intimate and insistent as that. The land exerts itself and has its effect. I'm roughed up or soothed, exhilarated or depressed, wholly prevailed upon from outside myself. I expected serenity, but I am labile and mood-struck. I change as the scene changes, as the sky clouds or clears. I conclude that nature is alive—if I hadn't known it before—and she calls the shots. There is no counter to granite escarpment or a sky pouring light. I went away to be with myself, but instead I'm in a protracted, uninterruptible encounter with the out-of-doors.

JUNE 18

I'm drooped in a swing in an empty playground in Shoal Lake, Manitoba, mid-morning, four or five days from home. Why it's called Shoal Lake I don't know. I don't think there's a lake in a hundred miles. I was lured in by the glittering new paint on the monkey bars and slide, the mauve public washroom with yellow roof, turquoise picnic tables askew in the shiny grass. Even the parking stumps have been dabbed intermittently by some light-hearted townsperson with a bucket of paint.

I'm adrift in thoughts of Bree. She'll be writing her exams. I saw her graduation outfit before I left, a flared black skirt and creamy white blouse, as if she were going for a job interview.

When I told her I intended to take a three-month trip, we were having coffee near her school. She doesn't live with me. To do her final year of high school she boarded with a friend in downtown Toronto. My partner Leon—my former partner Leon—and I live in a schoolhouse fifty miles away, where we've been since Bree was eleven. We tried to entice her there when we bought it. We painted her room, put down silvery broadloom, hung sliding glass mirrors from Eaton's on her closet. I found riding stables nearby and signed her up for lessons. She never moved in. She was living with her dad in Toronto in those days and disapproved of me buying a house with Leon and moving away. She would visit, though. She'd come on the commuter train as far as Ajax and I'd drive over the rolling farmland to meet her and bring her north. We got to know the landmarks on the drive: the fruit stand with the garage-size papier mâché apples out front, the ski resort that never got enough snow, the collapsed peonies in the cemetery, the solitary old maple where Bree once had me to stop the car while she buried a necklace, as a token, to find again when she'd grown up. Those long car rides helped us cling to each other when we didn't have a home together, held us captive to each other through her teens.

On the morning I told her I was going to drive to the Yukon, she looked out the window of the coffee shop at the streetcars chattering by on College Street and after a while said, "I've had this picture in my mind of a house—it's where I live with you, the picket-fence kind of house. My bedroom's always kept the same, my stuffed animals stay on the pillow, my books stay on the shelf, everything waiting for me, and I leave you, not you leave me."

People think that because it's common for families to break up, children must weather it okay, but I don't think they do. I work with families for a living, and for their sake and for mine I've held out against the idea that breakups are apocalyptic—but they are. For children, it's an atom bomb going off, no matter how tactfully parents manage it. Family life, whatever the quality, is the medium children live in. They're not separate from it. An individual self that can prevail, that can withstand change and loss, is a wobbly construct at the best of times. It's theoretical or, if it exists at all, must come sometime later. Maybe by middle age we have a self. In a child it doesn't exist. A child has no skin. When the adults come asunder, the child does too. They just do. I know this mournfulness in Bree.

But she's eighteen now, interested in independence herself. After a while she shrugs and looks at me, light in her eyes, her empathy for me swimming up. "Go on, Mom," she says.

I hoist out of the swing and get back in the car. I'm disoriented. I've lost my bearings on this enterprise for the moment. I didn't expect to fall out of the trip and into memory like this.

I HAVE TO DECIDE. I'll be in foothills tomorrow unless I turn off, north or south. This is deep prairie now, deep poverty, the place all in. I pass a faded baseball field, the diamond barely traced, the batter's net drooping on its poles. I see abandoned farms, the houses black and hollow, marooned in cut wheat as though their owners just walked away. There's a hovering, dusty poverty here.

The day is breathless. At Langenburg I decide to head for the badlands at the bottom of the province, a grassland region, pristine prairie, the land so hard and poor they never bothered to plough it. I leave the Yellowhead Highway and drop southwest toward the Qu'Appelle Valley, driving straight through the heat with a stop for lunch in Esterhazy, a square, four-street town, blank and dazzling as Mexico. This town is another world, the café white and glaring in the sun, trucks angle-parked at the curb. I get out stiff and shy, my Ontario plates and big plans embarrassing in a town so poor no one's going anywhere. The patrons of Esterhazy's air-conditioned café are teenage moms feeding their babies french fries and young men propped over coffee, chain-smoking, the sexes strictly ignoring each other. I order chop suey, which is not the gummy dish you'd think. Chinese Canadian restaurants in even the dinkiest towns out here interpret chop suey as fresh vegetables, barely stir-fried, with steamed rice.

The restaurant is cool and shady after the fry-pan prairie. Some boys across the aisle ask about the bike on my car roof.

"Where you going to ride that?"

"Oh, the west coast. When I get to the ocean."

"Bike won't do you much good out there."

I KNOW I'VE REACHED the Qu'Appelle Valley when the land drops into an east-west bowl, the bottom full of water and blurred farm-land, the hills a splay of knuckles down either side. The valley hums in mid-afternoon sun, broad and spacious, and I drive with all the windows open, stopping every few kilometres. Climbing up a scabby ridge, I can see the valley roll away along the Qu'Appelle River, the ground around me grizzled with tiny, wind-clipped flowers, wiry shrubs in bloom, glacial rock hazed in lichen. I climb in the soft air till my car is a dot.

It's a blissful afternoon. I take pictures of bereft farmhouses and, like everybody, try to figure out what it is about the light. Prairie light washes down, streams white, incandescent, from the whole sky, rather than flowing from a particular sun. At eight o'clock tonight it lies down in sheets across the land. Men out on their tractors make long silhouettes on the black earth, the dust behind them cartwheeling prisms in the slanting brilliance.

At Estevan on the hem of Saskatchewan I get directions to a big park out of town, clipped and flat like a golf green. I put up my tent beside a hedge, the only cover. This is a prairie phenomenon: every bush and tractor and human is visible for miles. When I hunker to pee, the car and I are the only shapes, horizon to horizon.

I search for half an hour this evening, but I've left Leon's camera case in the stubble of a farmyard hours back. The loss affects me inexplicably, like a rebuke. I lie in the tent trying to read, but my nerve has gone. I am utterly out of place here. All of a sudden, being on this trip is something I can't account for. It seems an act of desperation, completely arbitrary. What have I done?

ONE OF ALICE MUNRO'S collections of stories has the theme of women in the middle of their lives letting it all go, not gradually but in a single gesture. All at once they burn down the whole town. All the details to that point—the house, the marriage, everything accumulated or endured—is thrown over at a stroke.

Is that what I've done?

In my life some steadiness has come undone. My girl is coming to the end of high school. My partner has come unstuck from me. I felt change coming for a long time, like wind driving over flat land, some great undoing. I thought if I held still, it might sweep by me, I might get lucky in a buffalo stampede. But when it came, it bore right down on me, and now I can't stay still. Some exertion is called for, some self-rescue. There has to be some action from me now, a totem for these endings, a whirligig of my own.

This is why I'm here.

And the freedom to do it? How can I just close up shop and leave my post, leave my daughter writing her spring exams? That has an old root.

It was the way the loyalties worked with Bree and me, and with her father, though this is history and it's hard to tell true history. Bree was four when her dad and I split up, and gradually she joined her father's camp. I don't know why she thought she had to choose—maybe to make sense of the break, a child's way to deal with something incomprehensible. Or maybe simpler. She saw he was angry and she thought if we'd all stayed together, if I'd stayed, he wouldn't be angry. I think he offered her an explanation of what happened and I did not.

I didn't have a side. Not that I told her. What could I have said to a four-year-old? "I'm lonely, Bree." I thought that was beyond her and unfair to try to explain.

I don't see it that way now. In any break-up there's a dispute at heart and what I think now is that Bree needed to hear both sides. She needed to hear from both of us the love story and what happened to it—not so she could choose, but so she wouldn't have to. There would be a sad mom and a sad dad, and children can understand that. Small children can handle complexities of that kind. When Bree was in daycare, just a little girl, she told me one time about something that had happened with a friend. She said, "I'm happy about it and I'm sad about it." At three or four she could manage contradictions. But I gave her no explanation for the split, I didn't mention it, and when she was six or seven or nine, she took his side.

My version is pretty simple. I married in haste. I chose a person I didn't know very well. In one of her stories Lorrie Moore says something about who you marry being like the old game of musical chairs: when the music of being single stops, you sit down. At twenty-five or so I thought it was time to settle and get going on a baby. I married a person I wasn't suited to.

I don't know what his view of things was. He thought I was feckless. He was mad at me, and Bree fell in with his point of view. She kept a light, testy rein on me. I was her mom, but I was suspect. One time she was sitting in an armchair in the kitchen of a house I rented for us, small in the armchair, her hands up on the arms while I made dinner. "You live in joy while he lives in sorrow," she told me.

I stayed away from remarks like that. I kept quiet about her dad, and I didn't ask Bree how it was going for her or say how it was going for me. My reserve put her in a vacuum. If I had it to do again, I'd handle it some other way; not make her sort through adult umbrage if I could help it, but talk to her. As it was,

I blacked out the most important thing on her mind—the whole aching business of learning to be bilingual, bicultural, in two households—and with this ban on discussing everything vital Bree and I lost each other in a certain way. Gradually, very slowly, I fell out of feeling indispensable to her.

JUNE 20

I'm in a sort of expired rodeo grounds near Wood Mountain, Saskatchewan. No dew on the prairies. When I set my foot outside the tent this morning onto dry grass, it was as if night had never come. My tent pegs yank out dry.

Here's where Sitting Bull hightailed it from the Black Hills after Little Big Horn, a rolling, cowboy place without trees or features, just the spilling sound of meadowlark and wind.

I had a walk that bewitched me last evening in the furry hills, the grasses shivering and glistening at sundown, the breeze mild and dry. It's shortgrass prairie here, the hard dirt still holding last year's bone white blades. Filigreed lichen crawl on the cracked ground. There's sage and tiny flowers, stones like eggs and a hundred songbirds surfing the air. One kind makes a quick, wind-whistling sound like something coming undone, and there's a splashy black and white marauder—a magpie. I'd love to see a bluebird.

A museum nearby records that five thousand Sioux came here with Sitting Bull in 1877. There were no buffalo left and the North

West Mounted Police hesitated to extend rations to such high-profile Indians, so after three years Sitting Bull was forced back to the United States with those of his people who hadn't starved to death. I saw their photographs yesterday. Even half starved, their demeanour is exalted. They must have died appalled and gladly. The arrival of whites in North America is the dirtiest story in the world.

On the drive this morning I notice a local habit of disposing of car wrecks in the cleavage of hills. I see hawks, serious on fence posts, and deer, their white tails oaring the air as they run away. Swallows skirt in front of the tires, all of us under a moodless, unremitting avalanche of light.

WHEN I REACH the Grassland Preserve, the land changes at once. It is bluer, due to the native blue grama grass, and has a different configuration of rocks. These are scattered as the glaciers left them, not hefted into borders to make fields. Unmistakable as soon as I pass the wire boundary is the quality of wilderness— the atmosphere of freedom and quiet that always attends undisturbed places. The land rolls to the sky absolutely blank, earth and sky in flawless geometry.

It's the driest place I've ever been. I park and prep myself as though entering the Serengeti. It's noon and there's not a whit of shade. I pull out a hat with a brim, a long-sleeved shirt, my water bottle and wellingtons. The boots will be hot, but I'm thinking of rattlesnakes, wordlessly diagrammed on a sign as I drove in. I start walking southeast. Juniper bark crackles underfoot; otherwise there's not a sound. I photograph the deliriously overdressed boulders. Six, eight kinds of lichen in gold, orange, magenta, emblazon a single rock. Where life is impossible, that's where lichens go to it. I walk slowly, stunned by the heat and vibrant peace.

The grass grows in bursts, slivers of old stems, uncropped, ungrazed, meshing with the new growth. I smell sage and see my car with its felled bicycle glittering on the horizon. Buttes are all of a height, flowing to the horizon. Coulees, clogged with willow, scoop between them. Occasionally I pass a circle of stones, ghostly teepee anchors from the last century.

I spot a meadowlark in my binoculars dressed like a tiny leopard, his beak flexing like scissors. He flies off sputtering and erratic as a butterfly.

When I leave, I go to Val Marie, a dust-coated little town a few kilometres from the Preserve. There's a heap of ancient car parts half buried in the dirt on the outskirts, and the surrounding copse of spindly willows that all these towns have. I think the trees are planted as a gesture against the wind, a veil, a faint intercession between town and prairie beyond, between people and the ineluctable wind and desert, still ringing with Indians.

In a cavernous cinder-block café on the only street, I have canned soup ignited with black pepper. The owner has a worrisome pallor and sits smoking dispiritedly with a friend. She wants to sell the place and move away.

TO REGAIN the Yellowhead Highway I turn north, the air husky with smoke from forest fires burning north of Prince Albert—a familiar phenomenon this time of year. CBC radio matter-of-factly recites the conditions: "Swift Current twenty-eight degrees centigrade, with smoke, Saskatoon twenty-nine degrees centigrade, with smoke . . ." I drive briskly through the smog in an atmosphere of pre-storm gloom.

This evening at the South Saskachewan River past Swift Current, the air turns moist again. I pitch my tent on the delta in a grove of trees gently raining mysterious pale green petals, then recross the river to walk in the valley. The surrounding hills are close and smooth like a commotion of dinosaurs under a drop cloth. I walk toward them, following a deer trail, and see pronghorn antelope pogo-sticking up the slopes in retreat. I stay till the light is gone, the sun a sinking ruby orb in the smoke.

JUNE 21

I like these fragrant trees, the branches sweet with invisible singing birds. When I walk out to the river, there's something wrong. The water looks unnatural, inertly mirroring the hills. I find out later that the South Saskatchewan's been dammed and cannot flow—like a breast stopped up. Of all the trouble people have caused the land, the outrage to the plains is the worst—the rivers dammed for power, the grasses gone for fields, the soil broken and blown away.

The radio says there's a forest fire the size of P.E.I. burning in the north. The sky's invisible and cool. North of the river the land turns greener, flatter, amenable to ploughing. I think about the pronghorn last night, coming down to the water in the evening to drink as they have always done, though the river is fetid now and cannot move. There is something bleak about the animals' long habit, like hopeless loyalty.

It's past noon when I reach North Battleford and turn west.

Highway 40 is a less-travelled route from the Battlefords to Cut Knife, where Poundmaker fought a famous battle. He was a Cree leader destined to parley with whites at the end of the nineteenth century. The story goes that when Poundmaker couldn't persuade agents at Fort Battleford to help feed his people, some of his warriors stole provisions from the homesteaders around the fort. An incensed lieutenant from Swift Current led an attack on Poundmaker's camp at Cut Knife on a spring morning in 1895. Poundmaker understood the dim view whites take of desperate acts and was expecting the reprisal. After a six-hour scuffle, outnumbered and ill equipped, the Assiniboine and Cree managed to drive off the soldiers. Poundmaker let them retreat but, reckoning it wasn't over, took his people to Batoche to join Louis Riel. When he learned that Riel had fallen, he gave himself up at Battleford. He was convicted of treason and felony and sentenced to three years in Stony Mountain prison—this man whose ancestors had never seen a fence, let alone been penned. He was released within a year, his plight coming to someone's notice, and from the prison gate he walked to Alberta to stay with his adopted father among the Blackfoot. He died in Alberta within the year. He was forty-four.

In the 1960s, in some sort of gesture, the government moved his bones to his home at Cut Knife, to the site of the battle he unexpectedly won, now a quiet hill lightly decorated in his honour.

I come in the evening. The place is unmarked and I locate it by driving to the tallest rise, the most likely place to make a stand. There is no one around. The view on all sides looks out on hills and willow bush, the battleground marked by a large wavering circle of whitewashed stones. Within the circle is a Christian tombstone inscribed with Poundmaker's name, along with some Plexiglas photographs on mounts and two outhouses for visitors.

In the photographs the whites look fanatical and choked, their collars appearing to cut off the circulation of blood to their heads. The Indians look stricken, their eyes averted from the camera, a baffled, stinking hopelessness in the fall of their arms. Poundmaker is very handsome. While I stand there, a bluebird lands on his grave.

That night I sleep in a farmer's field nearby and, in the dark, coyotes call one another from the coulees around me.

I'M PARKED off the road a few hours east of Edmonton, sitting in the back seat with all four doors open to the breeze, writing in my journal.

When she was fourteen, Bree had a falling-out with her dad that was like bad lovers throwing in the towel. She was in her first year in a big downtown high school. I was fifty miles away, in the schoolhouse. She'd been shifting her point of view about her dad and me for some time; not so black and white, not so hard on Leon and me. We were making a little group, the three of us, jelling into a trio with some routines and comforts. I think she liked to be with two adults, not always paired off with one. The first year with Leon, when she was ten or eleven, we'd roughhouse with her, wrestle her down on the floor. She'd be half standoffish, half irrepressible, and she'd shriek as if something long pent up was getting out. At about thirteen she started nursing some grievances about her dad. She told me she'd made a list in the back of her diary— "Things My Dad Promised and Never Did"—the usual teenage reappraisal, but I think she couldn't change the deal with her dad. He couldn't flex, couldn't put up with her disenchantment. An ordinary fight went haywire. After some protest from her, something minor, he locked her out of the house. Probably he only meant to

scare her, but Bree wouldn't parley. She phoned me from my
mother's, declaring she wasn't going to live with him any more. So
I got her back. When she wouldn't come to the schoolhouse to live
with me, I went to the city and stayed with her wherever we could,
at friends' or at my parents', trying to get a lasso on her.

She came back in the visceral way I'd known her when she
was a baby. I breathed her. I tracked her in my cells. I'd wake ten
minutes before she came through the front door in the middle of
the night. I did everything in my power to summon her to me. She
came back hurt and stunned, and for weeks she wouldn't go to
school or say where she was going and I had no influence to steady
her. She had to reinstate me first. She had to change her mind.

Eventually she let me choose a good school, where she could
board, where she wasn't with her father or with me, and in a year
or so she came round.

Maybe that's why I thought I could come on this trip—because
she's all right now. We got to shore. She's got some confidence and
we have our old bond, the one we made going around with our
chests pressed together the first year of her life.

JUNE 22

Alberta. Wrong and strong.

Quite a change. Geographically, the land is starting to bunch up
and roll. The terrain is wetter, there are fewer grain elevators, and I

start to see those iron bipeds pumping oil, like automated robins ducking for worms. Oil is in the air, a faint, pervasive smell. In the towns I pass, pulp and paper mills stick right out, no attempt to hide them at a tactful distance. As I drive north into richer country, there's a push to get at it, to extract what the land has. This is a province on the move, more prosperous, more appearance-conscious. The auto wrecks flecking Saskatchewan, combed into coulees to disintegrate, are deployed as lawn ornaments here.

I have it in mind to stop in Edmonton before facing the Rockies, a last chance for cuisine. I reach the city limits about noon, stalling a few minutes in a gas station to collect myself. The proprietors seem harried, and the smell of oil and hot asphalt are like signals to raise the neurological deflectors. Just a few hours ago I was squatting over my cereal bowl in rosy prairie stubble; now I'm working hard to gear up to concrete and big enterprise.

Edmonton has two one-way streets bisecting the city, each a four-lane stampede past any stop or errand one might have. To get downtown, drivers are herded at breakneck speed past mile after mile of shopping malls—colossal Food Citys, Saans, Canadian Tires. As soon as one monstrosity ends, the next begins. Chain stores and restaurants have found a spawning ground here. How many Arby's can one town use? It occurs to me that the world's largest shopping mall could only be in Edmonton; here is the guzzling Texan mentality that would build it. Heading toward the city core is like a cattle drive. I'm nearly paralyzed with nervousness.

I find an Indian restaurant I have to pass three times before I have the verve to make the driveway, only to discover they stop serving lunch at two o'clock. My nerves are so flayed I find myself slapping at the glass door, imploring the surprised waiter to give me lunch. He does. I eat a meal I'm too disoriented to taste in an empty air-conditioned room while the manager, in a dim corner, tallies the noon take. Then I beat it out of town.

At Edson—*whack!*—there are the Rockies, like icy teeth on the horizon, sudden as fate. Out of nowhere the land leaps up and turns to rock. I drive glumly north, away from the sight, to William Switzer Park, a wilderness campground draped on a moraine beside a clean highway.

JUNE 23

Something I notice about car trips is the stretching and contracting of time. A hundred kilometres through one place is not a hundred kilometres through another. Ontario, for example, is much broader than Canada, the metal-loaded rock having its way with time, dragging it out, hauling the traveller to a near standstill, whereas the prairie frisks by, the merest reprieve, tucking up into Alberta foothills in no time. One is barely lulled, has barely started basking in the big skies, when the grassy sea buckles and bangs into the Rockies and it's back to gritty, skin-grazing rock. Nothing to do but be consumed. The mountains box out the sky, and British Columbia snags the traveller for days in its twists and turns and gorgeous views.

It wasn't easy to leave the kindly plains yesterday and drive into the mountains. I took elaborate precautions against bears last night, locking even my toothpaste in the trunk, then lay worrying about my minty breath.

Today I'm behind the first ridge of mountains, and there's surprisingly little traffic on a Saturday in late June in postcard-land. The weather's fitful and so am I, longing to see someone I know—anyone. I stop in the gravel by the side of the road, completely ringed by mountains so impressive they must be fake. Green-and-black water jitters in front of me. A loon passes, calling, overhead. There was one this morning where I camped, swimming solitary on the lake, just a trace of sliding wake, playing or practising. I watched him for twenty minutes or more. He'd beat his wings, rise like a phoenix splattering arcs of water, claw across the surface fanning and sputtering furiously, drop down and settle into flawless swimming again. Then he'd water-run again, repeat the whole commotion, till at last he climbed the sky and flew off down the lake, loosing that unearthly cry.

THROUGH THE ROCKIES, Highway 16 follows the Fraser River, a jade green ribbon looping west through alpine valleys. I drive all day in meadows waving daisies and Indian paintbrush and, after a long gas-stationless stretch, pull into Purden Provincial Park, a spruce and hemlock forest with a proper Saturday-night crowd. I find a campsite backing into dense bush, and when my tent is up I put on my bug hat and take a walk. There's a spicy sex smell of pollen in the air, and I see the lake has a fine scuzz of gold dust. Little by little my car is covered in it.

A tent and an ordinary car are the exception here. British Columbians interpret weekend camping on a different scale. They've come freighted with the comforts of home: campers that puff up into living rooms sprouting awnings and Astroturf steps, motorhomes equipped with generators to power microwaves, TVs and hot water tanks. I glance in a tiny window as I walk by at dusk and, sure enough, there is the blue eye. Outside are scooters and bikes, lawn chairs arranged under tarps, twelve-by-sixteen mesh tents rigged over picnic tables. Sheltered under these contrivances are rotisserie barbecues, propane lamps, camp stoves, coolers the size of doghouses, twenty-litre water barrels. Motorboats, squeezed ingeniously into the sites, bristle with fishing gear. I notice a practice of keeping a leaping campfire going at all times, even if everyone's inside.

Tonight I lie in my tent reading up on no-trace camping, including a chapter on defecating in the wilds. I sleep wonderfully in my purple cocoon and dream of being murdered.

JUNE 25

I am descending today, car and river tilting into the ocean, accompanied by Garnet Rogers's soulful fiddle music in the tape deck. Tonight I camp on Lakelse Lake, 145 kilometres from Prince Rupert, the end of the line. The climate's turned coastal, the air thick and moist, the vegetation maritime and right out of hand. Devil's claw sports leaves the size of placemats; spruce and cedar soar to the sky. There's a red beach by the lake, the mountains on the far side lost in cloud. I get up on a picnic table and sniff the sea.

I've been out here before. I came to see friends in Victoria a year ago and, spewing black smoke out the tailpipe, drove their ancient van up to Pacific Rim Park, a rind of trees on the west coast of Vancouver Island, one of the last temperate rain forests on earth. The eye-popping size of things out here is almost cartoon. It's as if the whole coast is on steroids, every living thing pumped colossal by the climate. I recognize the trees, these spruce and hemlock, the long-skinned cedar and its way of spinning on its axis. But trees back home nurse on acid soil and rock and wait out winters six months long, while these coastal relatives are doused in rain and mild sea air year-round. They grow six times the size.

This place clobbers you with the environmental message. The living world is on such a scale you can't miss it. The city gardens burgeon in February, shrubs improbably green, bushes stuffed with flowers. Vancouver has a downtown park that's a marvel of the world.

The destruction is unmissable too, the procession of logging trucks pulling timber out of the mountains, the mountainsides a patchwork of clearcut, the deals and hypocrisies plain to see. The first time I saw a logging truck on the highway hauling its booty—coastal timber, the live cuts huge and wet—I cried. You'd think the wretched chainsaws would wilt in the loggers' hands confronted by such trees.

I spent a week out here and went home swooning. A fabulous place with disaster on its mind.

JUNE 26

I reach the coast with a day to spare before the ferry crossing to the Charlottes. The kayak trip leaves June 30 and I have some time to nose around.

Rupert is a blustery town dealing in fish and softwood, the stink of pulp and paper wafting up the coast and sticking to the wet air. The iron docks, driven straight into rock and sea water, are testimony to the insane dauntlessness of pioneers. Prince Rupert looks like it shouldn't even be here, the whole town clinging to a soaked, black mountain.

I like it. The rain-slick streets ripple uphill from the dock, fast-moving skies push in, the atmosphere is bracing and rough—a port town with a hard-used beauty. My guidebook says it's Canada's most northerly ice-free port, a depot for halibut and salmon fishing, and for marine traffic up and down the coast. From here you can take a ferry across to the Queen Charlotte Islands or go north up the Alaska panhandle or south to Vancouver Island. I'll be doing all three before the summer's out. This is where I'll leave the car for the next six weeks. Prince Rupert is home.

Prowling around, I find everything I need: a Haida museum facing out to sea, a muddy campground near the ferry dock, a fish restaurant on the wharf.

WHEN MY TENT is pitched in the usual throng of motorhomes, I plod through town to visit the museum. There are posts in the yard, totems with the strong, sleek cuts, the crowded, bulging shapes the whole world knows. The Haida collection assembled here is my first encounter with an Aboriginal artistic culture strongly in revival. Inside, the objects of a hundred years ago are mixed with modern elaborations on the same themes and designs. A century-old serving bowl is placed beside a sharper-featured version carved a year ago, their proximity spanning the rent that history made. Haida artistry, faltering for a century, now comes back strong.

My reading about Haida Gwaii says the islands were named the Queen Charlottes for an English king's consort who never laid eyes on them. They've been the homeland of the Haida for thousands of years, a dagger of islands out in the choppy sea, famous for sheer cliffs and ferocious storms. In their time the Haida were a fierce, exalted people, "a people apart," Leslie Drew's little handbook calls them, raiding their coastal neighbours in open boats, rich enough, well-fed enough to outleap the drudgery of physical survival and build up an elaborate culture. Their wood, metal and argillite carvings are renowned. There is one of their canoes in this museum, enormous but graceful as a wing. All their tools and implements, the villages themselves, were made of cedar, endlessly adapted, the bark woven into all-weather garments or bent into watertight boxes, the tree trunks fabulously carved and erected whole in front of the houses, offering homage and defiance to the sea. The Haida used prisoners rounded up from their raids along the coast for subsistence tasks. When the Europeans came, they traded fish and fur for iron tools, using English wedges to push their art even further, till smallpox put an end to it.

I stand in the amber-lit rooms of the museum and try to envision their lives. Strength was prized. The young women would run backwards on the cobble beaches to build up their legs, racing each other. I can see them, their smooth, hard legs snapping back, their hair blown over their faces, throwing themselves against the low, dark sky.

Prince Rupert is a white man's town, built on fish and trees, but the centrepiece is this museum, a live heartbeat in a place thrown together for commerce. The totems in the yard, animate and exotic, merge with the fog and take the violence off the raw lumber.

TONIGHT I'M IN the clutches of anxiety, worse than when I left home two weeks ago. It's focused on my car. How can I move out of my car and walk onto the ferry tomorrow with nothing but a backpack? I glance around to see if anyone else in the campground is in this predicament, scaling down, pallid with fear, but the couples and families nearby look possession-fat and oblivious. My car is parked by a picnic table, never suspecting I'm about to leave it and virtually all its contents in it in a Quik-Mart parking lot for six weeks.

Before I left Ontario, I read up on what to take backpacking on the coast, and part of my quandary now is trying to get that small. The touring company will supply food and equipment, but I've got to think about clothes and weather. I found a book about travelling in the Northwest geared to the exposed traveller—long on thermodynamics and short on restaurant ratings. The authors described the fog-soaked mountains and fjords of the panhandle, stressing drizzle and sudden cold.

As for equipment, I'd had to upgrade. Over the years I had acquired an arsenal of homey, low-tech camping gear: bulky cotton and down items, perfect for sunny Algonquin canoe trips, feather sleeping bags patched with Elastoplast Band-Aids, cashmere sweaters speckled with moth holes, a shapeless canvas rucksack that pushed me to my knees on portages. This inefficient gear had great charm for me, as well as mishap-repelling powers that are hard to pinpoint. I hated to part with it. I was impressed, though, by what I read about feathers clumping when they're wet and the convection powers of the new synthetics. My reading recommended a polyester sleeping bag for the rainy coast and polyester apparel to "wick away" sweat. Even with the force of science I was slow to convert. Garments with these -phyll and -tex labels are chemical confections, repellent to a generation devoted to wool and feathers and a whole earth. In the end, though, the lore of insulation, conduction and convection, the diagrams showing vectors of perspiration exiting through invisible breath holes, won me over.

In the outfitting stores back home I consulted experts my daughter's age, hikers and mountaineers doing retail gigs between treks to the Himalayas and the Nahanni. I bought a used three-pound tent from a woman upscaling to a two-and-a-half. She came to my office in Scarborough in a crash helmet and Day-Glo bicycle suit and we set up the tent in the parking lot. I bought an American-made cookstove that fits in the toe of a sock and a tiny stainless steel pot for one-dish meals. I chose a nylon backpack with an internal frame moulded to my spine and a vast purple polyester sleeping bag (which proved strangely luxurious wet or dry).

Deliberations over rain gear took the longest. I knew I would be in rain all day in the panhandle, so my dilemma was what kind of wet to be: wet with sweat in a sealed raincoat or wet with rain, eventually, in a "breathing" fabric? In the end a balky loyalty prevailed.

Bill Mason, my old canoeing hero, wore a sealed rubber raincoat in *Song of the Paddle*, and so would I.

Into my pack in the Prince Rupert campground, for better or worse, I put my tent, groundsheet, sleep mat, voluminous new sleeping bag. No pillow. I take Eddie Bauer silk long johns, an old cashmere pullover of my father's, a caramel-coloured gabardine shirt, nylon wind pants, heavy-weight cotton shorts, Kettle Creek long pants (strong weave, dirt-resistant, shape-keeping), yellow neoprene rain gear, face cloth doubling as towel, thick wool sweater with zipper, underpants, wool socks, shoes to wear in camp, sun hat with brim, wool toque, mitts, bandana.

There is just room for a small toilet bag carrying Band-Aids, aloe gel for burn and bites, arnica tincture for bruises, my journal, and one precious book, Barry Lopez's *Arctic Dreams*. I also take a belt pack to wear in the kayak, containing a Swiss Army knife, three metres of nylon cord, sunglasses, scribbler, pen, and a bottle of sunblock around which I wrapped several turns of duct tape.

Everything else has to stay—all the miniature cooking utensils I am so attached to, all my favourite clothes, books, tapes, pillows and scarves.

Graham Greene writes, "The more bare a life is, the more we fear change." I had only a few items on the trail; now I have to go even more spare. I go to bed with a lump in my throat, setting my travel clock for five o'clock to catch the morning ferry to Haida Gwaii.

Two

LEON

I met Leon in therapy, the perfect place to meet someone. You know what you're up against. You know who the other person takes after in your family and what dilemmas you'll be reconstructing. That's the way with attractions. You never fall in love with a stranger.

This was not therapy therapy, with a professional, a stranger. We were a group of old friends—old lovers in some cases—all of us working as therapists and therefore obliged to have some kind of grip on our blind spots. We met one night a week in one of our basements, a rec room with carpeting and Indian print pillows and bolsters propped around the walls. Collectively we paid a fee to Madeleine, the one of us who had the most skill. Her job was to keep us to the rules and direct the dramas that were the therapy part.

The format was from theatre. We re-enacted scenes from our lives, recent or long past, that were awful or unremitting in some way, events or relationships that wouldn't calm down. We assigned parts and lines to one another, true to memory, then played the scene with as much emotional force, as heightened and dramatic, as possible. The idea was to fire up the feelings we'd had at the time and would have expressed then if we could have, if it had been safe or we'd had the wherewithal; if we hadn't been children, most often. The other players would be as provocative and exaggerated as possible while staying faithful to the text. Hopefully, the provocation would produce an emotional response, "a blow"—the bigger, the better—and the protagonist, in the safety of the situation, would let go expressively, let herself be fully angry or heartbroken, whatever it was. When we were worn out howling and pounding on bolsters, we would repair the scene, play it again the way we would have liked it to go. It was tremendously noisy and unrestrained and, I think, did us a world of good.

The theory is, if emotional safety can be established, if a person is not worried about being punished or judged but is free to go ahead and express emotions with great sincerity, the psyche is unburdened. Long-held emotions are drained off and the person, in a pliant, exhausted state, is receptive to a new experience, one that repairs the original. This repaired version has power. It comes as balm, and when it comes, lasting change is possible.

Creating the safety to work this way is the main thing. In our group that meant no judgments. If we had a reaction to something

another member said—which we did all the time—we had a format
for dealing with it. The reaction you were having was about you,
not the other person. We negotiated everything. We endeavoured to
ask for what we wanted and gave allowance to others to say no.
There was a value on non-coercion. Everybody took responsibility
for their wants and for getting them met. It was how we wanted
to behave in all our relations, not just within the group, but it took
discipline. Taking offence, second-guessing, laying blame, are such
normal, comfortable manoeuvres, it was hard to give them up.

This was my lexicon with Leon. It was our scaffolding for
dealing with each other. When we were arguing, we'd switch to
this training like a second tongue and carry on, with murder in
mind maybe, but at least blocked from saying awful things to each
other. It was like being members of a small club. This vocabulary
bonded us and set the rules of conduct.

MEETING LEON in therapy, I had his history, vividly, very soon.
He grew up in a small town near Chicago in the fifties. His was
one of the few Jewish families in town, a conditioning he offers to
explain the way he sets himself slightly counter to where any
group is heading.

He was the middle child of five. His father owned a store,
employing the children as soon as they got tall enough to reach
down stock. Leon was the younger son, the scrapper of the bunch,

the one who took the heat, the strongest. No one in the family took his side. He thought it was because no one liked him, but he found out later his father admired his spunk. His father, Albert, tells a story about a time when Leon was three years old and ran across the yard where one of his parents had just planted grass seed. His footprints were clear in the soft dirt. When Albert got home from work, he asked Leon if he'd been through the yard. Leon eyed him and said, "Did you saw'd me?"

Disappointed children often become self-sufficient, hard-to-please adults. Leon is one of those. When I met him, he was making his living as a cabinetmaker. The margin for error in cabinetmaking is one thirty-second of an inch. Leon applied that kind of rigour to everything. You couldn't beat him in an argument. His memory was flawless, his common sense relentless. He told me he'd been critical without mercy in his twenties and was easing off by his mid-thirties, when I met him. I hoped this trend would continue.

The first time I met him was at Kristie's, where we held the group. It was my first night. I'd been in a bad accident the year before, riding my bicycle, and I still walked with a cane. When I saw him in the hall, he looked like a storm coming, quiet in the eye, a slightly built man with broad hands and feet, black eyes and a blue-black beard dashed white at one corner of his mouth. He has a long, pale skull, bald since he was twenty. I said, "Boy, you're handsome," and he frowned.

I watched him in the group. He was the King of Swords, inter-jecting, protesting every inconsistency, every assumption—partly to distinguish himself, of course, but an apt habit, useful to the group. We had some early feminists among us. This was 1981 and every-one regularly put their foot in their mouth. All of us ran athwart these two women sooner or later—except Leon. He never said a clumsy thing.

I endured the barbed wire. I learned to pick my way. I grew more careful, listened better, and not just with him. And whatever you can say about someone, the opposite is also true. Leon soothed me. Back of the barbed wire was a zone I gradually got to know, a relaxed region, an unworried calm at the core that he must have been born with. As much as his ferocity drove me crazy, his phys-ical presence calmed me. He was fat for my nerves.

I remember a quarrel with my sister, a rare, terrible fight in the kitchen of a cottage we were staying at. Jesse is another one like me in the nervous wreck category, and we were taking a pounding. The only way I kept my head at all was that, over her shoulder in the living room, I could see Leon roughhousing with her small son, merry as could be, oblivious to catastrophe. He knew we were battling; he just wasn't worried about it. Most grades of tension are subliminal for him.

What attracted him to me? That's harder to know. The answer he's given over the years—that I gave him room—sounds like faint praise. When we met, I'd been laid up for a year mending crushed bones. Maybe I had a sheen of vulnerability at the time that was appealing in a headstrong person.

WE GOT GOING right away. We declared our attraction. We went away together over New Year's to the property Leon had bought in the late sixties when he first came to Canada, a bush lot at the top of Algonquin Park he somehow held on to when back-to-the-land ran out of steam. We retell this date, our first date, over and over. By now we have identical recollections; what we remember and what's gone from memory is the same for both of us.

We drove up in winter dusk, the afternoon waning fast that time of year. Already there was heaps of snow north of the city. We talked all the way, me next to him on the seat of his truck, so glamorous that old Chevy, a wool poncho drawn over the seat, the truck bed in back rigged with a frame he'd built and covered in a canvas tarp. I had my hand, in my mitt, on his leg. We weren't lovers yet and the prospect was zinging around the cab like lights.

The alternator on the truck broke about fifty kilometres south of the property. We waited in a little town on a frozen lake while the garage sent to the next town for parts. We went for a walk beyond the sidewalks. I lost my boot breaking trail in the deep snow, and Leon, behind me, grabbed my arm before I set my foot down. It felt strange to have someone catch my balance, someone

close enough and paying attention. We walked in and out of the
light from the street lamps in town, Leon telling me about coming
to Canada, evading the draft to Vietnam.

We got on our way again late and arrived in pitch dark, the
road full of snow, no house lights anywhere. We parked where the
snowplough had stopped partway up a hill, heaped our groceries
and bedding on toboggans, and trudged on, the exertion and freezing air a shock after the trancelike warmth of the cab. The moon
had not risen, but the snow lit a faint tunnel we could follow
through the bowed trees. When we stopped for breath, the silence
swallowed us. Hundreds of acres of frozen trees fanned around us.

There was a dark house finally, a hulk in the trees. No one
had stayed there for years. Leon undid the padlock and we went
inside, the air no different than outdoors. He put a fire in the stove
and lit the hurricane lamps. The room jumped up: a wood stove
in the centre, a rough counter along one wall, a box couch on the
other, some open-backed stairs leading up. When the fire in the
stove caught, Leon went back down the hill for another load. I
stood in my coat and mitts making soup on a camp stove, shadows flaring on the walls. I'd married him already.

IT'S STRANGE to think of him from here. That duplex wedged
downtown where we all met, where I met Leon, years ago. The pale
winter house where we first stayed together. I lie in the dark in my

tent on this far coast and it seems the present has nothing to do with me. None of this dense coastal history has anything to do with me. I'm in exile here. I see I've undertaken some self-banishment or self-dramatization on this trip, out here on the final ledge of ground before the continent falls off. So strange to think of him, to be inside a thing for years and then walk off and look at it from this far rim.

WE HAD A GOOD BEGINNING. Beginnings are thrilling, gorged with vitality, rigged that way on purpose, I suppose, a vestige from the early days of the species when mating had to be strong to keep him facing tigers, to keep her chewing hides and nursing babies.

Our first year together we slept at Leon's place, or at mine, or apart. He liked dark, soundproof crawl spaces to sleep in, and when I first knew him he'd fashioned a thickly draped ten-by-twelve cave in the basement of the house he shared with four other people out by High Park. His room was moonless, dawnless, pitch-black.

I lived communally as well, with half my therapy group and an occasional passer-through who stayed in the basement. For nights she spent with me, Bree had a bubble-gum pink room on the main floor. I slept at the top of the house in a white room under a slanting roof. One wall had a door cut in it with a tiny porch that overlooked our Portuguese neighbours' riotous back gardens.

We were happy. We stayed in bed in the mornings telling each other everything. We stayed in bed for about two years. We were talking, we weren't making love. Sex worked okay, but from the start it was a zone well out from centre. We were not devouring each other, we were not appropriating every cranny of each other. I wanted to. Like everyone, I wanted love to be effulgent, immoderate. The sideline place sex occupied from too early made me sad. I took it as a secret failing. I found I couldn't bring it up with Leon, and then it grew invisible; but that small lassitude between us grew pernicious. Like a spot on a lung, it made a hole in us.

He passed it off. Leon said he was tired of being led around by his cock, glad to be with somebody where the first thing wasn't sex.

That sounded okay. Mature. When you're newly in love you don't say "Oh, baloney" the way you will later on. Everything your lover says sounds plausible. Now I don't think so. Now I'd say sex is the bond-fast, the belly of mating. If it's incidental, there's a way the two of you will never find each other. Leon's meagre lust offended me in some way I passed over, incorporated. I could not bring myself to challenge it. Someone more confident would have, but I was not sexually brave. I did not go after him, look for ways to inspire him. I let it ride. For us, sex was the trap door under the carpet.

I suppose we always pick deftly. It may be that Leon and I did not want the prostrations of love. What we were up to together—psychologically, emotionally—may have stormed enough walls; and in the way couples do, we colluded that sex would be our holdout.

AFTER A YEAR we made a plan to spend the winter in the cabin we'd gone to on our first date. I'd finished social work school and wanted to take my time before I looked for work. Leon had savings. Bree was in grade six and living with her dad. She'd visit at March break. We made a couple of day trips to the property around Christmas to prepare. We asked the neighbours' help and hauled in a better wood stove, dragging it on a sled behind a pair of Clydesdales, their breath blasting the freezing air. We found some big preserving jars under the house that I scoured and filled with beans and rice. We scrubbed the floors and countertops, sanded the splinters off, mouse-proofed an old green chest upstairs, and beat the must out of the blankets. On the first of January, in the dead of winter, we moved in. Leon told me he thought he was moving there for good. He brought all his tools and books. He thought he was finally home.

For me it was winter camping, the house a brace of heated walls against the cold. It stretched out as far as I could see, as far as I could imagine: boundless cold, endless frail trees frozen in the snow. In bed at night I'd hear the ice in their limbs groan and crack, and everything about it was a luxury to me.

Leon cut our firewood with a swede saw, sawing and splitting outside the door for hours, thickening his arms and chest by the day. We fetched water from the creek in pails, smacking the ice open with the butt of an axe. I made meals in a soup kettle that we added to over the week, a never-ending stew. We took sponge baths in an enamel pan, limb by limb, stripped down by the stove. Once a week we'd take our laundry to town, an occasion to start the truck, dazzle ourselves in streets and stores, be around people.

Bree came. We bundled her and babied her, read stories and made sketches of the cats. In a knoll near the house we all built snow forts, taking the whole day. Leon's was a jutting wedge like a ship. Mine was a resolute wall that took more and more reinforcing till it looked like a ramp. Bree's was a starship, many-roomed, with a secret key to the ammunition. We were at it all day and then pelted each other with snowballs from behind our walls.

A game Bree loved involved tossing drowsy houseflies out the second-storey window. The cold would knock them to sleep mid-drop, and Bree would dash outside to retrieve them inert on the snow and carry them back inside to revive.

Her policy was to ignore Leon, but she couldn't keep it up. She liked staying with us, liked the huge outdoors and falling stars.

It was a fierce time, the most vivid Leon and I ever had—our marrying time. We still talk about it. Part of the intensity was how physical it was, every detail of the day requiring some effort, some exertion. I have perfect recall of that tall, over-warm, square house, pale in winter light, bursting with Leon and me. I smell birch smoke and wet wool, sudsy dishwater, soup. We were on top of each other and we stormed all the time, but the direction in those days was always deeper in. Over those three months we laid down our tracks. We had all the fights that would eventually drive us off each other, and we fixed them in all the ways that would knit us, keep us liking each other.

Leon's habit of acuity made him a keen observer of me. He knew me the way no one ever had. He held the mirror steady and I had

to be accountable, not to him—he wasn't like that—but to my own enthrallment. I wanted his esteem. I wanted my own. It's the power lovers always have over each other. In his company my colourful opinions had to start standing up for themselves, pass muster. I'd shoot off some long-held view and find myself taken seriously. I loved his querying and I hated it. I resisted him and then quit resisting and began to learn from him. I stopped second-guessing. I stopped flouncing off to end an argument. I started to fight fair.

WE WENT HOME in March. We knew we would. The next summer we looked for a place of our own, some compromise between city communes and the woods. We found a schoolhouse in a ghost farm village fifty miles from Toronto. It was an hour and a half from the job I had taken but as near as we could afford. The property was an acre trimmed in old spruce trees. It had a brick schoolhouse set back from the road and a huge steel garage. Leon put a big Quebec stove in the garage and set up his woodworking shop, and I made the drive to my counselling job in Scarborough.

The house was a hundred years old, roomed off at some point after its schoolhouse days. It had a bell tower on the roof, six tall round-top windows facing east and west, and a huge beehive in the back wall. An old fellow came into the yard one time and asked about the hive. He told me it had been in the wall when he used to come here as a boy attending school. Every spring a few stray bees would stagger into the house and I'd trap them in a glass and carry them outside.

The yard had an old perennial garden with heavy beds of peonies and phlox, pure yellow day lilies flopped over the pump, and a clump of huge mauve iris gone silver with age. Rusty hollyhocks grew along the wall. A line of dusty Norwegian spruce separated us from the neighbours and lay thick bands of shade across the yard by mid-afternoon.

I kept the flowers going and planted herbs. My mother gave me dogwood and forsythia bushes the first spring, and Leon put in a post fence to circle a vegetable garden. The wire he used was so thick and taut it could have kept in wild horses.

It was a funny house indoors, all grey corners and wavy linoleum. We bought it without going inside, if you can imagine, peering in the windows on tiptoe. We never took to the inside of the house. I don't think we ever really moved in; we were happier pitched in the yard. A friend came after we'd been there for years and noticed the pictures still ranged along the floor, no nails put in.

For one thing, the partitioning was never right. The rooms were inexplicable, and there was a full-length false ceiling that lobbed off the windows halfway up. In a spare room by the stairs I hung red drapes and a clothes rod and laid my best possession, a handwoven rug. I couldn't think what to do with the room after that. We had to swivel sideways in the bathroom to get between the sink and the washing machine. The living room was too long for people without furniture and had a lurid green rug we eventually stopped noticing.

We slept upstairs in a vast attic with the original plank ceiling arcing over the floor. I started scrubbing the old paint off one time and got about an eighth of the way before I left it, a clean beige square over the bed. We made the mattress ourselves out of layers of cotton, gradually creating a boundless cotton raft that got away from us, lunged off the platform and spread like caulking foam. We never could find sheets to fit it.

Bree's room was a different story, outfitted with broadloom and mirrors and a real bed, a different vintage entirely from the rest of the house, and, as it turned out, unoccupied. She never moved in. She came weekends with a backpack and spread her things on the floor as if she were camping. As time went by I gradually took it over, easing a few winter jackets into the closet, sleeping in her bed on airless summer nights.

We were there seven years. I dreamt about it the other night. Someone else had moved in. There was a powerboat in the yard over my tulip bed. The perennials had vanished, shaded out, and the vegetable garden was a kerfuffle of weeds and tall grass, clamped by Leon's peerless fence. Leon, a ghost of Leon, was squatted in the driveway weeding the gravel, preoccupied and patient, working his way through planks of late sunlight down toward the big maple at the road.

THE HOUSE HAS THE PRINT of our journey in and out. In the first two years we dug the vegetable garden, renovated Bree's room, stripped the wallpaper in the living room, knocked a wall out in the kitchen. In the last few years we didn't change anything. Leon made himself a lair upstairs, a bunker of heavy desks, which he piled with books and computer paraphernalia. I established a region of selfdom up there as well, a den of bookshelves and piled rugs. Our sleeping came unfixed. We abandoned the vast futon, both of us drifting around the house, usually together, but not designating a bedroom. We began to stay away nights after days in the city when it seemed too far to come home.

WHEN I COME HOME from this trip, we won't live in the schoolhouse any more. We've decided to sell it. Leon is doing a different kind of work now, learning a model for conflict resolution. He sold the cabinetmaking business and doesn't need a shop so much. He found it lonely and wants to be around people more. The last year or two, he's been away weeks at a time.

Bree is finished high school and wants to travel.

I'll move up north to the property we have—I call it ours now, the land we stayed on in the beginning. I won't go to the house we lived in that first winter. There's another house, a more kept-up one with hydro and a basement. I'll move there.

Leon won't come, at least not now. He'll make a base wherever there's work.

I THINK ABOUT the habits of that house, the one Leon and I bought. Six years of gardens, six rounds of phlox and peonies, purple and cerise, bundled in jars. Six basil and snap pea harvests, corn one time. In winter the scrape of the steel door to Leon's shop, Leon inside building tables in his work suit and felt hat, covered in sawdust. The smell of Bree's room, the unused cool of it. A hundred passes with the vacuum cleaner over the algae-coloured rug, a thousand armloads of stove wood. The huge safety and comfort of my relationship with Leon.

On this trip I need to portray our separation, to feel the absence of Leon as extremely as I can. That's what it seems. This is the vertigo between founding myself on him and founding myself on my own, and I want to get it over with. I'm trying to be pure alone, to have completely what I have anyway, the way an inoculation gives you a dose of what you're going to be up against, in hopes of a cure.

Three

CHARLOTTES, ARRIVING

The ferry from Prince Rupert makes a lurching six-hour crossing of the Hecate Strait to the all-tides port at Skidegate. Getting off the boat in the Queen Charlotte Islands is like stepping into a greenhouse, another world. The name conferred on it by a European captain in 1787 to honour an English queen withers at once. It must go by the name the Haida gave it: Gwaii Haanas, Place of Wonder.

To the left, winding along the shore, is Queen Charlotte City, a white town with a weaving line of frame cottages, a supermarket, a school and a baseball diamond. Along the shoreline to the right is Skidegate, a Haida settlement, one of two communities where the Haida pooled when there were too few of them left to maintain their villages throughout the archipelago. The place is a chilly riot of green, the air soaked with oxygen, the forest pressing on the settlement, growth gobbling up the backyards. Everything is jumbo size: devil's claw, foxglove, lavish berry bushes shoving into the road. I plod up the hill under my pack, sniffing like a colt.

JUNE 28

This morning in the museum by Skidegate, I met a man I talked with yesterday on the ferry, Hilary, with his daughter Mary. On the boat Hilary told me about the daughter he's visiting, how she left a high-profile job in Toronto to move out here, bought herself a used van outfitted with two captain's chairs bolted into shag carpeting, found a gut kayak in Calgary and drove to Queen Charlotte City. Now she lives in a house with the tide at her door. He didn't know how she'd make a living and was coming out to see how she was doing. When I meet her this morning, she's my age or a little younger, in rubber boots and a home-knit sweater.

The three of us stroll around the museum, a modern construction with vaulted ceilings and tall windows looking on the sea. The objects displayed are familiar: halibut hooks, bentwood boxes, carved feast bowls, animal masks, the bold, flawless cuts of Haida art. I stare at a grey photograph of a woman carrying firewood. She's on a dim beach, a row of sea-facing houses rising behind her. Her bare chest shows under a cedar-bark cloak. She has a stone labret embedded in her lower lip and stares through the camera at the person photographing her. At the time, half her village must have been dead.

In the afternoon, following the shore past Skidegate, I come upon a Native cemetery on a bumpy hillside and go in. These are Christian graves, a part of Haida history that came later, incongruous and sad in a place so wild. Most of the headstones are marked by blackened columns, some in low iron enclosures with ornamental Victorian posts, some engraved. *Chief Skidegate, died December 21 1892, aged about sixty.*

The place is tended in a rough way, the grass hacked by some kind of scythe. Clumps of spotted tiger lilies have been left to grow, their petals stiff and fleshy, salt-tempered. The air races offshore, tearing the high clouds in a brilliant sky. A bunch of ravens sail over my head and out across the road to a row of cedars backing the beach. The sea's way off at low tide and shows a dozen shades of blue, whitecaps kicking up out in the strait.

In Skidegate, Mary told us this morning, there's plenty of work guiding and fishing. Some people have the old carving skills and make art, elaborating and re-creating Haida designs. When I walk back, the road through town is empty, lined with prim houses, trucks and bicycles in the yards, wind chimes twirling on the porches. There are none of the usual residential postings, no SCHOOL ZONE or FOR SALE signs.

The scale must be why it feels good here. These huge beaches, quick skies and riotous vegetation run all over and people just tuck in where they can. Things are in the right relation for once, nature raucous and overgrown, humans cut down to size.

I know I'm romanticizing. This isn't paradise. A fifteen-year dispute in South Moresby taken up with the government by the Haida and conservationists to preserve the area from resource extraction ended just a couple of years ago. Much of South Moresby is now a National Park Reserve, spared from logging by the skin of its teeth. There are clear-cuts just south of here. But the inevitable is taking longer in this out-of-the-way place. There's still juice here, something wonderful, a compressed, bursting energy— the way the plants hop the fences and leap out of the gravel. It makes me want to spin around and yip.

JUNE 29

I lucked into the sweetest day today. I stepped into the road about noon and the "limo" driver who takes people from the airport on Sandspit across to Queen Charlotte City stopped when I stuck out my thumb. It's his day off and he's going up the coast to Tlell to have supper with his daughter. He said, "Come along."

Sergis du Bucy is seventy-three and, except for six months' military training in the forties, has never been off Haida Gwaii. He's a bony man in a white, buttoned-up shirt, with a beaky face and big pale hands. His manner is mild and friendly; he's comfortable with himself and used to showing people around. We follow a winding coastal road along the open Hecate Strait. Huge empty beaches roll away from the road and a big lowering sky makes the day portentous and grand.

Sergis's daughter, Margaret, has a bunkhouse backed into a dune on the Tlell, a bright brown river that fills with sea water on the flow tide. The landscape is entirely different from the misty fjords I'm expecting in South Moresby. These are dune lands—fine gold sand and tufted goat grass pale as jade, wild tansy.

Sergis settles in to visit and I wander off, making my way over a barricade of beached logs onto a colossal shore bulging into the low sky as far as I can see. Gulls clamour under the cloud cover and, in the distance, sandpipers twinkle along the surf line. I head north toward the glowering horizon but gradually get drawn in by the watercolour stones underfoot, smooth and subtle as eggs. Finally I'm bent double over them, stopped. I collect a little company of black, plum and copper ones, and a snowy clamshell, and wrap them in my windbreaker.

Margaret includes me in a cold chicken supper with homemade buns and pie, this wonderful fare somehow emanating from a place without power or water. Her air of resigned courtesy suggests that her father regularly shows up with complete strangers. We talk about living out here, the seasons. "November's the month you'd like to be someplace else," Sergis says contentedly. Late afternoon we take our leave.

On the way home Sergis points out ranchland, uniquely low-lying, and tells me there were homesteading efforts at one time, now mainly petered out. We stop to investigate a dead whale, peach-coloured and mournful, washed up on shore, and a boulder the size of an outhouse, balanced on an edge no bigger than a breakfast tray.

When we're back in town, we top things off with a visit to the dump to watch the black bears snuzzing in the garbage for food. I tell Sergis my impression that present-day Haida are prospering here and he replies, "Well, that's fair. Makes it better for everyone. I couldn't have a good house and him have a bad one. You'd never feel right."

PACKING UP in the hotel later on, I try to prepare myself for the kayak venture tomorrow. The outing is unimaginable. We are to assemble on Sandspit tonight, camp together and fly out in the morning to the put-in place at the bottom of the islands. I have only the orientation package I got in the mail to go on—a what-to-bring list and an itinerary of the expedition. The trip is fifteen days. There will be two guides, non-locals with kayaking expertise and graduate degrees in some natural science. We'll travel every day, never the same camp twice, visiting the old Haida camps at the tip of South Moresby and along the sheltering east coast. We'll see the village of Ninstints on Skun Gwaii and, to the north, Tanu. We'll

be flown in and out by Twin Otter and paired in tandem boats—
"surprisingly stable" according to my "What to Expect" page. I'm
expecting to be among the least experienced, never having kayaked
at all.

I'm more depressed than excited. The inevitability of this
adventure presses on me, like being trapped in line for a Ferris
wheel ride, my ticket bought and paid for, the wheel swinging
overhead, closer and closer. I'm thinking how much I'd rather just
make taxi runs with Sergis.

Four

HAIDA GWAII

We are twelve, including two guides, Bob and Heather. The orientation package described Bob as "musical," a natural history graduate, with twelve years' experience leading trips in Haida Gwaii. He's in his late thirties, a fine-boned man in a plaid shirt who spends our first eight hours together frowning at weather readings and going over lists. Heather is tall, athletically glamorous, with a mass of red hair. There's one other Canadian besides the guides and me, a wiry school principal from inland B.C. A youth from Belgium arrives late, looking baffled, an expression he wears for the entire expedition. The rest of the group are Americans. There's a pair of women friends from New York, Rhee and Ann, a biologist and his wife from Utah, a woman on her own from California and two Jims, one a machinist from Las Vegas and the other an advertising executive from Washington state. Most are outfitted in brand new Gore-Tex and neoprene booties. None of us has been in a kayak before.

We met last night in Sandspit, a tiny settlement of general stores and bed and breakfasts on a low table of sand sticking into the Hecate Strait, flat enough to land airplanes from Vancouver and Seattle. This was our departure point, halfway down the Queen Charlotte archipelago. A seaplane was to carry us to the southern tip of South Moresby early this morning, but the day came up low and blowing, heavy mist drifting over the airstrip, blocking visibility. We waited all day for the clouds to lift, the group getting acquainted in the canteen without me. I have no idea how to manage this, make friends with a group of strangers I'm about to be confined with for fifteen days. I stayed outdoors, roaming the gloomy beach, the small measure of readiness I'd mustered for this venture leaking away. By the time we rattled down the runway mid-afternoon, I'd lost all will to go.

When the plane lands in Rose Harbour, we climb warily onto the pontoons and make our way to shore. The kayaks are here, six double-seaters drawn up on the beach, looking incongruous. I have no idea how they got here. The place feels not only uninhabited but never inhabited. The air smells never breathed, the rising hills look uninvaded, no clearing or seam. The water shows every sunken stone. Bob says Rose Harbour was a whaling station, a white man's enterprise, and before that the Haida made it a summer camp.

Carrying gear up the beach, I notice tokens in the black gravel: coal and clots of iron from the whaling station, machinery filigree and ocean drift, a tiny shard of porcelain from Japan, huge chalky scallop shells, like cupped hands mauve at the wrist.

When we're all ashore, Bob flings six tent bags on the beach and tells us to pair up. The twosomes fall together, the Belgian student and I unmatched at the end. He takes the last company-issue dome and I unpack my Eureka.

Back of the beach is a lime green meadow, soaking wet, rocking with tussocks and tree stumps, a clearing that's barely holding out against the flow of forest. We put up our tents in grass so heaped and lush, the rolling ground beneath is no bother at all when we lie down to sleep.

Outside my tent tonight I hear water running under me and, in the dark, sink my toothbrush in the grass to catch it.

JULY 1

Today we paddle out of Rose Harbour after a demoralizing morning adjusting foot pedals and breaking down equipment into kayak-size bundles. I realize that all of my carefully selected gear is silly. Where can I stow a twelve-gallon backpack? What do I do with a Siwash sweater that folds to the size of a toaster oven? What to make of bulging cotton socks that take three days to dry? It's evident to me now that this trip is about getting wet and quickly getting dry.

Bob squinted up at a certain point in his routine this morning and picked me as his kayak partner. A nose for a fellow introvert is my guess.

Through the morning the weather stirred around and changed its mind till it seemed unlikely we'd leave at all. I'd wandered off down the beach when I heard Bob yelling to heave the boats into the water. After hours of standing around, suddenly we're off.

The sensation is startling. A kayak is not a canoe. Rather than gliding on the water, one is *in* the water, reconstituted as a seabird or water creature, a sleek swimming pod, part of the circle of sky and sea.

These big tandems are blessedly steady. At least, I feel steady, paired with a maestro and freighted with the heaviest load. Stroking out of the silver bay is pure joy.

A dawning drawback, as we settle into a rhythm, is the constancy of paddling. I'm used to a canoe, to the long, varied paddle strokes and the practice of switching sides. In a kayak the stroke is unvarying. You hold your arms straight out, collarbone height, rolling your shoulders in an endless rhythm, levering out of your hips. My paddle is an uncontoured, oar-like shaft of heavy wood, unwieldy to the bitter end.

Before we leave the channel and tackle the open ocean, we stop for lunch, pulling up on a small rock beach with the usual background of lime green plush. Our blood's up and we're feeling relieved to be off. Heather digs out a Tupperware box that holds the perishables. Lunch will be the same every day: two slices of bread open-face, one with the special of the day, something like tuna salad, chickpea mix or tinned salmon, the second slice a filler of peanut butter and jam. We've each been issued a water bottle, stowed in reach under our spray skirts, to be refilled at passing freshwater streams, and a zip-lock goodie bag, precious as emeralds, full of nuts, dried fruit and a single Mars bar.

I eat happily and ease my back onto a flat rock that's almost warm. The sky's plain and kind. Before we push off I climb into the woods to pee. Bob advises that toilet paper pollutes and won't be offered. He suggests sphagnum moss, springy and slightly antiseptic, or handfuls of sea water if we're crouched in the intertidal zone—an ecologically sound place to defecate. This ritual isn't for everyone, but I come to like it.

It's another world when I enter the forest. I'm enfolded in the spongy trees, all sound absorbed, the place so zingy and oxygen-stuffed I forget everything and become simply a bunch of senses. I lose track, muse on the trees, inhale the vibrant calm of the rain forest. These are ghost trees, these cedar, spruce and hemlock, breathing old hymns. Moss covers their entire length, the whole forest stoked in velvet—a sanctuary, thick and humid and cool.

It occurs to me tonight that we paddled in the open Pacific today, onto the savage west side, ten inexperienced people who've known each other one day, out on the wild ocean in small boats.

JULY 2

I crawl out of my tent this morning, two moon snail shells the size of softballs glowing on the ground where I left them last night. The tendons in my forearms are hollering for more rest. The sky, edging toward clear yesterday, has a water-filled radiance. I sink my head in a stream, stained bright brown by the surrounding cedars, and clamber over drift logs like straddling a succession of horsebacks to get back to my tent.

I hardly know what to make of today. It is an astonishing day of sunlight and wonders and sorrow and fatigue and debris and discouragement and spirit world.

We leave our campsite at Fanny Beach and paddle out in the ocean around a flat rock called Flat Rock, riding the swells and watching puffins and seabirds whose names I try to memorize. Pigeon guillemots are the black, chubby ones with a white streak on their wings, and oystercatchers have very round heads and long red bills. There are many puffins, lovable natural comics. In flight they look like big cigars.

I'm enjoying the kayaks a lot. When we cruise up to an island or a rock, the water slops crazily back and forth, the boats somehow holding their own in the rambunctious backwash off the rocks.

I begin to have a rapport with Bob, which I would describe as a communion of silence. He tends to commentate briefly if he's making a decision: "Hmm, there could be orcas in that channel.

Let's check it out." Otherwise he shows no inclination to get acquainted. Within a few days I'm in the same cloud of private musing as I was on the drive out.

After circling Flat Rock, Bob catches a fish, whacks it with a piece of kindling, strings cord through the gill and mouth and tosses it on the deck. From there we go straight out to a mound of rock frequented by Steller's sea lions. Bob informs me there are big colonies further south. The dozen or so animals we see here are the outlaws and cripples—defeated bulls who lost the squabble over harems, along with some barren females and immatures. Exiles. We paddle closer to get a look. Their golden bodies are slung as though boneless on the rock. The air is a din, the atmosphere grouchy and charged. As our approach stirs them up, they start bawling and shouldering one another into the sea. I didn't expect to be so thrilled by animals in the wild. I didn't reckon on their power, the way they create a whole environment with their odour and noise and mood. We creep among them elated by their non-human presence, their pungent, unknowable life.

Then we rock and reel to the back of Skun Gwaii, where the village of Ninstints still stands. Our expedition begins with the high point, a lingering Haida village, now a World Heritage Preserve, standing where it has always been, a treasure of history. Because of the wind we cannot approach the beach front-on but must park in back of the island and hike to the village over an old forest trail. The Haida took the first trees, but even this second-growth is formidable, the ground around the trees snaggled and torn as though from huge seismic shifts.

I cannot enter the place. When we come to the cove where Ninstints stands, I stay back in the trees, stunned by the presence of spirits. The air in the place strums. I have to sit down and watch from the edge until it grows more neutral and I can go in. The village stands in a small gravel cove, a crescent, the silver remains of posts tipping at angles around the beach. Afternoon sun lays shadow on the scurry of surf at the waterline.

Haida lived here. For thousands of years they fished and went on raids; for a couple more centuries they traded on this beach with arriving Europeans. Then they got sick and died, and those who didn't die had to leave and go up to Skidegate. I'm amazed to find the emotion of those events still here. There's been so little in the way of trespass to disturb or dissipate what happened. There was the trauma that soaked the air with adrenalin and grief and then a hundred years passed like sleep, and now we enter in the low afternoon and find the poles still sighing.

The quality of quiet is so deep that one by one we stop talking and sit down and lie down, and finally we are all lying in the moss in the old village and a few deer come in and begin to eat.

JULY 3

A thing that is troubling me from time to time is the ethics of our being here. When we're in these camps at night I think how troops of us pass through every summer, and no matter how no-trace we try to be, we make an impact.

When we're dicing onions tonight I ask Bob why he does it. I know he loves the land, but these expeditions are hard on it. Why does he take people stomping through the old forests? He gives the answer I've heard before.

"People coming on these trips are often travelling in wilderness for the first time. Hundreds of inexperienced people sign up every year to be escorted beyond habitation—to paddle, trek, fly into places like this, the world's last places. The physical world is powerful, but it's also fragile. My hope is that travellers who come will be changed by it. The exposure will get to them; they'll go home more conservation-minded. They might change some habits, take a different side in an argument, write a letter. That's the hope."

He's bound to say this, but it's not a rationale that settles me. We still leave our mark, we still disturb little and big circles of life. It's the slow death rather than the quick one, is all. I know wild places die faster by chainsaw and strip mine than by the gentle harassment of the wilderness business, but the outcome is the same.

LAST SPRING was the first time I came out here. I was in Tofino on Vancouver Island, and on a rainy day I took a tourist boat—a coast guard boat with room for twelve—up the coast to visit a hot spring. Away we went, zipped up in red spray suits and navy blue toques like a brace of bowling pins, myself and eleven German tourists. We roared north, keeping well out in the swells, and on the return we meandered through the little coves along the mainland. Puttering into one tiny bay, the guide said we were entering a favourite nursing ground for a certain kind of shark. He thought if we were very quiet . . . and I thought, "Oh, sure. A tourist season five months long, two trips per day, this company alone—we're bound to come upon sharks raising their young."

That's the rub. People want to see wildlife in their secret nests and dens raising their young, migrating, sparring for territory. People want an orca to leap over the bow of their kayak for their camera, but the more we press wild animals, the more we drive them off. Tension grows between the expectations of clients who've paid so much to get into these places and the needs of wild creatures.

In testy moments I think, this is what consumerism does. It turns everything into product, habituates us to look for a certain kind of value, dims our recognition of the real watering holes. Dropped into wilderness, we act the same as we do rating a pricey hotel. How thick are the towels? How many grizzly sightings?

Consumerism hones the powers of appraisal and discrimination and shrivels the capacity to be content. I think so. To be in these last places, these last wild places on earth, paddling along, living outdoors—that ought to be enough. As it is, we expect the day to go beyond itself, to cough up a sea lion or a snorting orca in front of us because we paid so much and it was so awkward to get here.

I ram a tent peg into the moss and notice a problem with my righteousness. I'm one of the ones who goes home inspired, one of the enthusiasts Bob hopes for, but I also come back as often as I can, and every time I do I scrape the lichen off its thousand-year-old grip and alarm the pronghorns drinking at the river. I alter where I go, modestly deface and wreck it, and so do thousands of other keeners; and if this is nothing compared with the chemical sewage pouring out of Marathon into Lake Superior, I stand by my point, hypocritical as it may be. I don't quite think we should be here.

WE BACKTRACK TODAY through the pass at Rose Harbour to get to the east side of the archipelago. The rest of the trip we'll be blocked from the open Pacific, tracking north along the leeward coast through the relatively protected waters of the Hecate Strait.

This morning was a hard paddle, and I distinguished myself by staggering out of the boat at noon and shouting on the beach, "I HATED THAT." My hands are swollen and my tailbone aches from bracing against the seat. We are human hinges out there, straining fulcrums between water and wind.

We camp early and pass a hot, fine afternoon on a short, crunchy beach. I go off with the women to bathe in a glen, our white, moundy bodies bent in green light in the stream. There's a seal playing offshore, its exhalations loud when it surfaces.

This evening I walk back of the campsite into the woods and notice in the thick quiet the absence of birdsong or scuttle. Bob says there aren't many animals, just a few black bear and a small kind of deer. The only thing I see is banana slugs. Overwhelmingly it's trees, these old, moss-caked cedars, standing or toppled, sopping up all sound, the whole place like a sponge, gently, implacably filling.

Conversation floats back from our camp on the beach, people propped against drift logs after dinner, getting acquainted. The group is taking shape. Cathy is one of those migratory Americans who's lived all over. Lately she's from California. She's gregarious and generous, the one who extracted all our biographies and links us. She paddles with Jim from Seattle, handling his razor humour with unflagging good temper. She and Jan, the school principal, tent together, attending to each other in a practical, easy way, like a fold-up marriage.

The couple from Utah, Mike and Pam, are Mormons; shy, unassuming, gently walled off from the rest of us, paddling, eating,

tenting together, complementary in everything. Even their percep-
tions are shared: "We wondered . . . We think . . ."

The Belgian student paddles with Jan and sleeps by himself. He's
out of his element both by age and by culture, virtually mute. I can't
gauge what he makes of the trip. I have a fantasy he's on the wrong
trip, that he meant to sign up for an oboe workshop in Vancouver
and found himself here, too baffled to speak up. The two Jims have
adopted him in a gruff way that both demotes and includes him.

Jim and Jim are tent-mates, already the strongest force in the
group. They didn't know each other before, but they are a fit. Jim
from Seattle is an advertising exec, strapping, pugnacious, a master
of sarcasm. He has the American trait of exaggerated self-esteem
that Canadians find vexing. The other Jim, from Las Vegas, is a tool
and die maker, relaxed, absorbent, sly, a tireless foil. These two give
every campfire a kind of edgy energy, one Jim delivering feints
with his wit, the other chuckling and blunting the barb.

Rhee and Ann are housewives from New York, long-time
friends, self-assured. Rhee paddles with Heather, the other guide,
and Ann with Vegas Jim. They've done this before, gone off
together on adventures, and know the ropes. They have steady,
unflappable pacing and enviable gear: pastel bug suits, functioning
dry bags, effective skin lotion.

Heather is an apprentice guide. This is her first trip with Bob.
She moulds herself to his leadership perfectly, skating in sync with

whatever he's up to. She's strong, deft and shy. She and Bob tent together, join each other in every task, Heather smoothly putting flesh where he's lean.

JULY 4

How many days out? Four? My hands want to split out of their skin. They're hot and swollen from clenching the paddle, the backs glazed and salt-baked like fired pots. Last night I walked up and down the beach gripping a cobblestone in each hand for their soothing cool. I'd pace, heat up the rocks in my palms and set them down for fresh ones.

We had a wretched paddle this morning out of Rose Passage and north into Hecate. I was searching every cranny of myself for some last cache of energy, glaring at the shore as it passed inch by bloody inch. Bob had the wherewithal to point out a bear somewhere ahead and a sea lion huffing in the water beside us. Eventually we stopped for lunch at an old camp, skidding on the steep beach as we pulled the boats up. My role in landing requires clambering overboard into the surf to lead the boat in, and the reverse when we take off—I tow us into the sea. I live in wet running shoes. This detail is a significant feature of the expedition, easily on a par with seal sightings, and ought to appear in the brochure: "Visit Abandoned Haida Camps in Wet Shoes."

While we napped in the shelter of drift logs after lunch, the weather changed. The sky cast over, the wind dropped and we went on in a different day, a hazy cheesecloth sky drawn across deep, easy swells. I sang sorrowful folk songs to myself.

In the middle of Carpenter Bay, in silence, in no current at all, we paused and drifted for a few minutes, falling into reverie, floating in a gossamer sky. This is the inside-out of the morning's wrenching exertion, the bliss on the other side of the moon.

Many times each day the splendour and solace sweep me up, take me out of the paddling and thrill me past anything. It's a ravishing place, like steering through live velvet. I am moody, though, a scrapyard of emotions, the welling and brooding a mystery to me since it isn't tied to thoughts. On this trip I don't think at all—the life's too demanding. My senses are pried open and I get tossed around.

At dusk tonight, in the woods far down the beach, standing in a triangle of trees, I'm gradually surrounded by chanting. Under the wind, slow but unmistakable, comes a far-off, solar-plexus-rattling ululation. Craning to hear, out on the water I see a night tableau, or think I do: thick men in gusty torchlight standing in their boats in the blackness, and on the shore a black surge of women, filling the air with singing. From the sound I catch a vision of Haida men putting to sea to fish or make war, and their women sending them off. Gradually the sight thins and wears away, though not the sound. After a while I come to myself, standing in the trees in the dark, and walk back to camp.

NOW I START to dream—protracted, hectic dreams that stay with me, distinct, when I wake up. This hasn't happened for a long time. When I was laid up for a year after my bicycle accident, my dreams grew huge, which I attribute to the simplicity of life as an invalid. Dreaming must be partly problem-solving, and, during that laid-up time, each day took so little to resolve that I had to go deeper for material, grist for the psychic mill. All sorts of ancient puzzles surfaced, in one disguise or another.

73

It's like that here. Each day burns everything to nothing. We work so hard breaking camp, paddling, setting up camp at the next place—always outdoors, always someplace new—there is no residue, nothing for the mind to pick at in the night. So I oar backwards in my sleep, find old reserves. The water and hills and sky imprint themselves all day, pre-emptive, and in my sleep, in darkness, my own life glides up, portrays itself, seeks consolation.

I'm dreaming about Leon. He's with me out here, where I thought he'd never come.

JULY 5

I turn in my bag, grey seeping under the slope of the tent. I slept poorly for the first time in a long while. The air is still charged, the Haida present, last night's scene electric. I feel like a tuning fork. To add to it, I'm pushing my body too hard. Every morning I crawl out of the tent not nearly ready for the day's exertions. This pace is not mine. I'm begging muscle and bone to give more, to catch up and build strength. I lie in my slippery bag at night and talk to my forearms like a coach in a locker room in the middle of a tough game. "Now, men, you can do it. Just get out there."

WE'RE OFF to a fragile start. It's a bright ride out of our cove, but the north wind assaults us as soon as we turn the corner. I'm in no man's land, wan and captive, and I paddle hard. The fragility wears off, my muscles warm and, as they take the bit, I stride out of the grasp of spirits. Matter over mind.

I cannot tell where the Haida tableau last night came from; whether it was a phenomenon outside myself, a ghost scene there on the water, arising from a ritual repeated so many times or so potent that it shimmers still, a hundred years later, for any overwrought person to see, or whether I imagined it, created the scene in the back of my own eyeballs. Bob, at least, believes me. He has seen ghosts and commiserates in his brief way.

Late morning, the headwinds drop. We get into a straggle of islands and headlands, and stop for lunch at the foot of a sheer hill. Our boats keep sliding back into the sea and we have to run for them.

I love the slack time after lunch when we crawl off somewhere behind a drift log to doze. My bones give over to the warm bank with its fizz of grass, and every thought empties into the ground, the kind of release you get only if you've been racking yourself.

Dead calm this afternoon. Paddling is tedious and heavy. Swells and currents, even headwinds, are better than this flat calm with nothing to brace against. "I need the wind to animate me" is how Bob puts it. I focus on my life preserver stowed on the deck, watch the dipping paddle blades out of the corners of my eyes. Paddling becomes yoga in this lull. I attend to the effort in my body, pushing away on the stroke, levering off alternate feet, trying to loosen my grasp on the paddle to save my thumb joints.

To ease the boredom, Bob rigs a sail. Not much air to catch, but it's fun, groping with another element for a way to meet and fit.

Behind us I catch drifts of conversation. It's the habit of the group to paddle within chatting range—the Jims and Cathy, at least. Bob leads, Heather sweeps and, if the going's easy, the rest bunch up and talk.

It's smart, this pairing off with a partner in the boats and tents. It fosters a buddy system, everyone having someone to look out for. The emotional needs of the group tend to stir around within these pairs, freeing up the leaders to navigate, fix rudder lines, lead.

It's stressful out on the ocean. We may be having fun, spiritually moved, loving every minute, but we're stressed. Under the exhilaration we feel the strain on our nerves. There is so much strangeness. In the mornings Bob pulls out the laminated sea chart and we crowd around, staring at the blue and white shapes, the course we'll take that day, but we don't really know where we are or where we're going. The map has nothing to do with the actual prospect, the shoves and pulls of the real ocean, the boundless sky and wheeling wind, the enormity of weather and tide and current with no handrail. Out here our routines and habits are blasted to kingdom come. The quirky comforts we've built up over years are gone, unreconstructible. After a day of newness comes a night of newness. Under the circumstances, emotional connection is crucial; someone to fuss to, someone to help you find your bug lotion.

I have no buddy and no bond yet with the group. My mood of exile—Rapunzel in the tower—keeps me off, as if I must do this, must let the land bear down on me, muse on Leon, stay apart. If I could start the outing again, I wouldn't do this. I'd avoid isolation, fake sociability, join in somehow. Paired in the kayak with Bob and sleeping by myself, I have no one but the landscape to turn to, and as a consort the landscape overwhelms me.

JULY 6

This morning started raw. I was dreaming of Leon. We had no home and no place to be together. Today my palm feels the back of his neck.

The day heats up and flattens out. We're floating through a skein of offshore islands, the ocean floor plainly visible beneath us, a waving lawn of empty clamshells and lounging starfish of every colour. Swaying among them is the concoction of some kind of snail, a whirl of glue and eggs that looks like broken clay pots.

This afternoon we make an early camp in a hemmed bay and, after setting up, venture into the live wall of forest back of the beach. The place is a den of filtered light and ancient trees on the verge of shattering. We clamber over seeping primordial stumps that collapse and crumble in our wake. Our shoes kick up divots of moss. Our exuberance makes such a path of wreckage, I'm glad when we go back.

Later, with the low sun straight in our eyes, we women swim off the barnacled rocks, stroking out in a lamé sea. A harbour seal rises beside us like a ghost.

WE'RE IN A PROTECTED ENCLOSURE back of Burnaby Island that was cramped and stifling when we arrived in the blankness of noon. Now, at low tide, the perspective has changed, the view wide and lifting. Fog muscles down the hills to the west like lava, sneaking under a clarion sky. There's wind in the trees high up, and seabirds cry around the empty bay. The beach has become a live museum, the out-tide exposing mounds of rock slathered in gold kelp. Thousands of barnacles cake the shore rocks, their mouths clicking at the deserting tide. Stranded jellyfish, like messy organs, gape on the wet stones. Ravens will pick them off before the tide flows back.

Tonight it's buckwheat and saltgrass for dinner, butterscotch pie, ocean on three sides, wind and eagles. Bob plays the concertina, stretched out against a log. Heather leads Cathy and Jan in some shy dancing in the cool sand.

THE KIND OF VEGETATION we get when we're paddling further out is bull kelp. It anchors in thirty feet of water, growing a foot a day toward the light in spring. We find it sprawling on the surface, the slippery stalks wrist-thick, rubbery amber-coloured streamers trailing out for yards. In heavy wind or current, we steer into a patch of kelp, grab an armload of these floating ribbons and hang on, anchored to the ocean floor. I like to handle it. I like the urgency, rocking on the sea, struggling to catch hold, to yank a bundle over the hull and get a cord around it just under the gas bulb, like choking a throat. Fastened to the kelp patch in the ocean, we can relax, stretch back in our seats, enjoy the tumult.

The paddling life is established now. There isn't so much preamble and milling around when we take off. Bob has discarded the tensor bandage he wore around his wrist the first few days and I've outlasted the hand-padding arrangements I used.

There's a joviality out on the water, a dome of good spirits whether we're paddling close in a pod or strung out. Our boat leads the way and behind us through the day, unless we're flat out against current or wind, I catch voices pitched light. There's a link between exertion and high spirits. Once the body is equal to the demand, the stress of physical effort works toward euphoria. Neurologically, emotionally, humans love a pounding heart.

Balancing the long, repetitious bouts at the paddle are the rests—the rollicking rests in the kelp beds when it's blowing, or the heavenly rests in flat water when the sky is gauzy and windless. We rip open our spray skirts and dig in the damp air between our knees for water bottles or candy. When the water's easy, we let ourselves drift, arching a little in our seats, letting our arms go slack, lapping up the atmosphere. Sometimes we see jellyfish straying by on some submerged, mysterious errand. One today looked like poached eggs.

We're changing, softening like pummelled leather. The experience of being here is intensely physical and emotional. The barrier we normally keep between ourselves and everything else, the filter that organizes experience, gets mashed in a place like this, where the trees are a thousand years old and the sea sweeps over the edge of sight. We're released from our lives with only what tokens and comforts we can cram into small bundles, and the work of paddling and bending and lifting all day dissolves our defences, drives us into our bodies and our senses. With the casing pounded thin, we seem more life-size, more human and susceptible.

On this trip I fit myself to the land in the most literal way, opening my skin to it completely. I lay my spine down on the ground and take warmth from the stones. I press my ribs and belly on the moss and the ground takes me to itself. I open my eyes like sponges. Live nature seeps into my body, blanks my mind and dismays me with her force. When the wind blows, I perk up; when we paddle in calm, I flatten. On broad beaches, my chest spreads; when we draw up in hemmed coves, I constrict. It is union with an overpowering lover, no different, I think, from the experience of being in love. My cells feel swollen and crowded, my nerves strummed. I am woozy and irritable and rapt.

JULY 7

Halfway point. Now I expect perfect consciousness, my body equal to the task, my spirits imperturbable. It doesn't go that way, of course. I spend the morning trying to think of ways to impress Bob and worrying about the gash in my toe that won't heal because my feet are never dry.

Bob is a big preoccupation. We all admire him for his skill and aloofness. He isn't unfriendly, but he keeps a reserve that's beyond professional, tantalizing to us women, of course—the hard nut to crack. It's obvious the place thrills him, and his excitement makes him spontaneous and open to the day. I think he took this job as a way to be in Haida Gwaii. Meeting people or being the leader—

even paddling—wouldn't be the draw, not after twelve years. He never seems quite involved in any of these activities. He has the look a mother gets sitting by the wading pool watching her toddler, the senses scanning, alert for mishap, the mind gone elsewhere.

Moiling around with Bob in the ocean all day, I'm used to him, but I am never easy with him. Our routine is to check in briefly in the morning when we first get paddling—tell a dream or an idea about something—then lapse into an all-day silence. He asked me the other day during one of these morning exchanges what my life was teaching me. The ponderousness of the question made me nervous; I hunted around for an adequate reply. Certainly I am taking life seriously, but at the moment, foremost in my thoughts is sheer thankfulness at being physically up to the trip; I'm delighted not to be a gibbering wreck by two in the afternoon. I mumbled something to that effect and felt myself drop over the horizon of his interest. Bob isn't a dynamo, but he is a set-up for fantasies, the way guides always are. All that casual skill.

FULL MOON. That means bigger tides both ways, filling and emptying. Accordingly, the carry to the water this morning is interminable. When we land for the night, we lug the kayaks up the shore above the high-water mark so the boats don't wash away in our sleep. In the morning, when the tide has been and gone, we carry them back to the sea. The feat of lifting loaded boats is managed one boat at a time. We pass five or six nylon straps at intervals under the boat, everyone taking an end, then hoist the kayak like pallbearers, and convey it to the sea. It's a precarious ritual; footing in the cluttered intertidal zone is death-defying.

Before settling into today's paddle, we hike through an acid bog to visit a drizzling savannah, a vista of tussocks and gimpy bonsai trees, dramatic in the rain. We like the change—this wide, sodden Africa after a week of sepulchral forests and sea.

When we take to the boats again, it's an easy six-and-a-half-mile paddle through a glassy black channel to tonight's camp. It's my favourite kind of camp: huge. To the west the hills we left this morning still huff fog down their sides. To the north and east the horizon is empty. Salmon jump in the dim surf in front of us, and along the beach giant clamshells, chalky and stiff with age, glow in the dusk. I take some of these. The perfect small hole at the hasp is made when the moon snail mounts the clamshell and uses its tongue to bore into it to extract the flesh.

JULY 8

Many trips to the intertidal zone this morning, my bowels premenstrual. On one of these trips a bee stings my calf and Bob ingeniously supplies a hemorrhoid suppository to shrink the welt. Mentally I add Preparation H to my "What to Bring" list.

Our muscles accept any job now, and we streak six miles across Juan Perez Strait to a cliff, which we ply around, lunchless, till mid-afternoon, examining the walls and fissures sloping into vaults of turquoise water.

Tonight's camp is a noble one: west-facing, the horizon well off and ringed with nippled hills. A cobble beach rumbles out of sight to either side of us, backed with drift logs and a vast lawn of moss and duff grazed dry by the sea wind.

I bathe with the women in a pocket of rock out of view. I'm menstruating and sit in the sun absorbing the warmth and letting my blood run down the rock. We've reached a point where the paddling doesn't take everything we have, where rest time is not filled with recovery. We have something left when the day's exertions are done, and it is the loveliest sensation. Time feels available in a way I've never experienced before, welling and rich, full of possibility. This is as relaxed as I have ever been, as free from anxious future-thinking as I have ever managed.

I get my stomach down on the baked round stones the way I've seen seagulls do. Out of one eye I see Mike fishing in the path of the sun and feel the breeze on the skin of my arms. All the women are menstruating, our cycles veering into a communal one and, having nothing else, I collect sphagnum moss to bleed into.

HAIDA GWAII is a waterfall for the senses but murder on us physically. I'm losing weight, which I can ill afford to do. "See Abandoned Haida Camps in Drooping Clothes."

I've developed a habit of working my hands every time we stop, every break in paddling, bending my fingers back to stretch and loosen the tendons. The damp air fixes my fingers into claws. All day my hands are basted in sea water clutching that unlovely paddle, and they swell, hot and sore. The shaft rides on my thumb joints, on two small, aggravated points of bone. Bicycle gloves would help, but I didn't bring any. I got blisters across both palms the first week and tried all kinds of remedies. I wore rubber washing-up gloves for a while, thinking they looked festive, but my hands hated being cooped up. I tried Band-Aid and duct tape arrangements that rubbed off. Mainly I just waited to toughen.

Legs are another casualty site. All day we bang into hard objects. I have tiny red punctures on the insides of my knees and nicked ankles where there is no flesh to cushion collisions. I've acquired chartreuse welts down both calves from scrambling in and out of the boat and jamming my knees against the hull during hard paddles.

My cotton shorts have a perfect bull's-eye salt-stain around the crotch from the steady leak of sea water through my spray skirt. There is always a cloying dampness below decks as I rock along in an eternally wet seat.

Everybody's footwear is taking a beating. Those who brought polypro kayak booties have shredded them staggering up and down the stone beaches under the weight of the boats. My feet, in blue running shoes, have been dyed bright indigo. My shoes are disintegrating; the rubber has come unglued and the suede is turning to mush. I'll get a last few days out of them by lashing the soles to the shoe with duct tape. My feet are dry only at night and look like light-starved ocean creatures.

Nobody minds. None of us cares about the discomforts. Some who came on this excursion can't touch their toes, suffer greatly from the regimen of sleeping on the ground, slamming into rocks and yanking on the wild ocean all day, but it's the same for all of us. None of us cares. By now we've all released, given over to the life of the trip. We've all fallen to the pulverizing, tenderizing effect that exhaustion and landscape have on us—the helpless bliss that pierces us.

The skies are often lavender in the evening. There are wistful sundowns, the sun taking leave without blaze or spectacle. I sit on the pale stones apart from the group and go into memory. I have no choice. There's no turmoil to it. I think that part was past before I ever came out here. What's left is having to remember, to bustle through the details for myself. Sometimes, sitting on the cobbles at sundown, I just tend memory. The scenes unreel, I watch and breathe. I take it as a part of leaving. I think it will be a long part.

JULY 9

This was a rotten day. We had two mishaps, and a hard rain that started at supper tonight is still drumming in the dark on our soaked tents.

The day began with a stop at a hot springs on a low island bitten by shallow bays. Mishap number one came as soon as we landed. Rhee fell on some slippery rocks and had to rest for a couple of hours bundled in a blanket on some boulders. While she revived, the rest of us lolled around. Bob and Heather donned wetsuits and went snorkel fishing, slowly duck-diving for half an hour, filling string bags. When they came ashore and dumped their catch, I went over to look. Abalone resembles female genitals. Out of water, its lippy body strains to flip over to its protected back. Sea cucumbers are nubby peristaltic tubes. Bob cut the head off one, squeezed out the innards in a bloopy flood and slit the body to get at the edible part, the pale strips of muscle that line the inner walls. Heather served up the creatures for lunch on the Tupperware lid, their flavours too subtle to detect.

We'd been anticipating the hot springs, a warm, freshwater soak after days of sticky sea water, but it was a luxury that fell flat. There'd been a one-time effort to domesticate the springs, probably from the days when there were whalers in the area. We trudged into the clearing over a slimy footpath and found a clump of wooden change rooms around the silty pools, dilapidated and smelling of rot. Maybe the dregs of habitation spoiled the springs. We submerged in groups of three or four, bodies wan in the grubby water, scowling for each other's cameras.

The wind was up mid-afternoon when we prepared to leave, purple clouds dragging in from the east, the sky lowering. We made a broadside crossing, losing sight of one another in the drops and crests of the swells, waves flopping over the decks. After a desultory morning, the change in the weather snapped us to right away. When we turned tail to the wind, the going got even more raucous, the boats champing and pitching, the waves hurling us headlong. Sometimes our boat lifted clear out of the water and I'd swipe air with my paddle. Bob rigged a sail while I kept us squared to the rush of following waves, and once we were organized I gripped the sail between my spread arms, catching the wind while Bob steered. It was an exuberant, careening ride that swept us into camp in minutes.

Just before we landed, mishap number two happened: one of the rigged boats dumped. Bob and I swerved to the rescue. When we came alongside, Rob and Jan had kicked free of their boat and were in the water gathering stray gear. Heather power-stroked to our away side and took hold of our deck to stabilize us while we flipped the overturned boat. Jan hoisted her way back into her seat, got her billy going and paddled to shore in disgust. Her partner, Rob, crawled onto my deck, his head in my spray skirt, arms and legs clamped to the hull, amid hoots from the cheap seats about bagging a man.

WE ARE CAMPED on a point on Faraday Island. There's an old garden here, gone to seed, awash in foxglove looking like a throng of bridesmaids. A thin, cold rain began at suppertime and everybody crammed under the tarp Heather and Bob strung up between the trees. Jan and Rob were chilled and rueful, probing their stuff sacks for leaks. At dinner we jostled for chili and warmth, anything that was going, competitive as crows.

JULY 10

I'm awake, though it isn't day. Probably the rain woke me, the slight anxiety the tent won't hold. The outside of my bag feels damp. I spread my rain jacket over it.

I miss the smell of my bed at home, the cotton futon Leon and I made. That mattress took maintenance, one of us separating and fluffing the layers every so often, pounding down the ridge that would rise between us. The bed took the print of us, two slight ditches, within a few weeks.

The rain on the tarp has a weary sound. I sit up and put my headlamp on and write.

WHAT HAPPENED TO US? The impossible and hackneyed question. I feel myself click into a practised reply. Let me avoid that and wrestle it some other way. When love ends, you probe for a long time for an explanation and after a while it's too exhausting to think about what happened any more and you sift down to some formulation, some bitter or blaming or incomplete idea you tell people. There's no truth to it. The live fish of the two of you has long swum out of reach and was unknowable anyway.

The undoing is so sad and monumental you think there must be a way to grasp it, get a rope around it, make it comprehensible, but I don't think there is.

What happened to us? I don't know. Maybe we lacked intention. For a while there was so much to do. We had to tell each other everything, read all each other's books, move in together, see Bree through her teens. We were swimming toward each other, and everything was toward each other, every effort to that end. Even fighting was to clear the way in.

And then what? Did we draw too close? Was I frightened when I saw him in full detail? Did I think he'd sink me if I got so close? This is the theoretical part, because I don't remember being afraid. Yes, I do. I remember panic in the fights—that we wouldn't get through it, that I couldn't reach him, soothe him, that I'd have to give my life. It felt colossal like that. Intimacy is regressive territory.

Maybe it was ordinary terror. Intimacy with another person is always terrifying. I suppose if you mean to be intimate with someone, it's a matter of living with that, being able to stand the oscillation between too close and too far away. At one pole you're fused with your lover, engulfed; at the other you've pulled back so far you're out of business together. The extremes are unavoidable, our thermostats ungovernable. The thing is to bear the emotion, the panic, at the far ends.

Maybe this explanation makes the most sense to me. The terrors of the deep. In my relationship with Leon I was frightened at the fused end of the pool.

Leon said he got tired after seven years—tired of working in the shop alone, tired of mothering me without being able to tell me how to mother him. What did he mean? I spread my dishes on the table; he ate sparingly. I wanted him to take what I had, what came easily to hand, not make me work so hard. This was our sticking point: his narrow receptivity, my anger over it. It set up an unclaimed, perfidious zone between us. He didn't tell me how to reach him; I didn't beg to know. I didn't try to guess. Our own peculiarity, perhaps, his hang-up paired with mine, a trouble particular to us. If we'd got help, perhaps we could have braved it and gone on.

Or not particular to us. Maybe we encountered a regular hazard of intimacy, a treatable dilemma. Maybe we reached an end to what we could risk that was only temporary, and accidently lost each other.

It seems to me relationships are works of imagination. I don't mean they don't exist, just that what we make of them is theoretical, a mental construction. The experience is real and compelling, but what you can say about one you're in is just a working hypothesis. It varies, it depends. It isn't the same as a fact. A couple says, "It's time to go," and that's one way to look at it. On the other hand, it might be time to stay, in a different way.

Leon and I couldn't rouse ourselves, couldn't decide. I have an image for our quandary. My mother gave me a cedarstrip canoe for my fortieth birthday, a lovely eighty-pound craft that is like silk in the water. For a couple of years Leon and I took it out. In Temagami one time, at the end of a day of paddling, we made a portage over a dam and got into a dispute about whether or not to leave the canoe overturned while we went back for the packs. It was pouring rain. This was a point of canoe etiquette. I have a picture in my mind of how we resolved it: a green canoe balanced gamely on edge on the gravel shore, on three inches of gunnel.

We were too long in this impasse. A space came between us, and though I don't remember it, the sensation of it, it must have been there, some black muck waiting for Leon at the end of his tether, for me at the end of mine. Or maybe it was nothing dreadful, just what inertia creates, held long enough. Just a cooling. And in this cooler place, one thing led to another.

I don't think we stopped loving each other. We kept talking. We have no arsenal of unaired grievances. Neither of us imagines ourselves hard done by. We just let the line go slack. We stopped wanting to do whatever we were doing together. It seemed to take too much of us. We stopped swimming in and started to back-tred. We saw the water widen and couldn't bring ourselves to stop it. Leon got interested in computers, bought himself one, dabbled seriously. About the same time, he started working with someone who had a method for conflict resolution, a man I introduced him to at a workshop. For Leon this was a way out of the woodworking shop and into his element, and he began to be away more and more, travelling with his teacher.

I didn't pursue these passions. I took up yoga and on weekends skied by myself in the hayfields around the house. I liked being outside. I wanted to take the canoe out more than Leon did, and it became a joke between us. I'd ask him to come paddling with me and he'd invite me, as a trade, to spend time on the computer. We'd let a little time go by, the choice would hang in the air, then we'd let each other off and feel grateful to be freed. I lay in bed one morning thinking about trading in my boat for something lighter, something I could lift by myself.

In the last year or so before this trip, Leon would be away for weeks, in the Midwest or California, learning this mediation work. I was restless at work. Maybe it had nothing to do with work, maybe I was at some depletion point. I was in menopause, yanking my sweater off in the middle of meetings, going blank mid-sentence.

I found a journal entry from December '87, two and a half years ago, sorrowful about Leon. Even then there was a way I couldn't reach him, couldn't tell the ways I was a pleasure to him or sustained him. I had started to resent him and close down.

Our parting took this form—not recriminations, not someone else. We crept into ourselves. I was afraid of change. I *am* afraid of change, and I held still, letting things drift. I did my yoga and it taught me I'm alone.

IN THE COURSE of my work I read about intimacy and autonomy in couples, and I like the idea that, if you last, you have to marry the same person at least twice. The first time is the easy one. You have being in love going for you and everything is the journey in, but you will encounter fear sooner or later—two years, five years. Somewhere the fusion, or lack of it, feels frightening and then you think about whether to stay or go. If you stay, if you remarry that person, it's a clearer choice this time. You make it more differentiated. You see the foibles in your mate and you know your own. You make a choice to abide with the flaws or fix them. If you decide to leave, it's the Rubicon uncrossed. You'll pick again, another partner, or you won't pick, and come to the same point.

For Leon and me, losing each other was arbitrary. I think so. We might have avoided it if we'd been willing. We came to the choosing time, the occasion to remarry. We chose. When I said

"Come paddling" and he said "Sit with me on the computer" and we did neither, we chose.

THE RAIN HAS STOPPED. At eight o'clock it's beatific. I feel quiet. I've worked this long enough. We haul the boats an all-time thirty yards over dry rock, then barnacled rock, then slithery sea lettuce, then a final welter of damp starfish and sea life.

Tide and current are in our favour out to the Tar Islands, and we hazard modest sailing with reefed sails. We rest up in a kelp patch in a very strong current, where Bob and Mike pull in a quick catch of rockfish.

We plunge onto a scarf of rock, shallow water scudding between dozens of low islands. Harbour seals surface shyly to watch.

Landing on a rock for lunch, we hunt for a spot out of the wind and eat hummus mix, bread, cheese, sliced pear, mashed salmon, peanut butter and jelly. I've started coping with the stampede at mealtimes by hanging back. Bob says we're the hardest group on jam he's ever seen.

Veins of tiny flowers are snugged in the rock. Bob says we don't see them on the mainland because deer knock them off, though when they're hungry, deer will make the swim, even out this far. A stunning image to me, deer churning in the salt sea.

To the east lies Lyell Island, the famous region that brought a moratorium on logging in South Moresby. From here we can see that the hills have been clear-cut, except for an old-growth swath around Windy Bay too awkward to log. The bay is so shallow, low tide drains it of water, making the shore unapproachable for hours each day. This is our destination, and we'll have to time it. We pack up, catch the tide and scoot over the water, weather and current altered again. We haven't had the same paddle twice.

Windy Bay is handsome. There's a bit of a settlement. A watchkeeper presides in a longhouse with two enormously fat women. Behind their yard is a big golden forest with a full stream, a labyrinth of deer trails and the usual mob of ravens. Bob is excited to be here and eager to talk with the old man. He cooks up a special meal, a "jum" of our catch this morning tossed into a chowder broth. For hors d'oeuvres he serves the watchkeeper fried abalone and sliced sea cucumber with a sprig of dill. The old man remarks courteously on the hunting, the salmon expected next month, the two-point buck one of the women—his daughter, it turns out—shot and canned the other day.

The bending riverbed behind us gradually fills with sunset, green and gold rills flaring up. An eagle rides down between the long trees, fishing.

JULY 11

By now I've worked out the perfect pack list. It's a comfort knowing what I should have brought.

For clothes:

2 pairs nylon shorts with liners

2 or 3 cotton undershirts or tank tops

2 broken-in long-sleeved shirts with collars, Viyella or cotton

1 pair fleece leggings, for evening

2 or 3 pairs wool socks

2 pairs running shoes: 1 dispensable, for the boat, 1 dry, for around camp at night

1 nylon pants and windbreaker with pockets, fitted at wrists and ankles

1 breathable rain suit. Sweat is a worse kind of wet than rain.

1 pair bicycle gloves

1 tie-on sun hat with brim, 1 wool beret for nights

1 cotton bandana, as neck-shade and washcloth

1 compressible jacket, wool or fleece, functional when damp

Give up on underpants.

For equipment:

• many small nylon stuff sacks containing zip-lock bags or— more expensive—several roll-top dry bags

- waist pouch, reachable while paddling, containing sunblock, lip balm, pocket knife, sunglasses, extra twist-ties, duct tape
- first-aid kit containing vitamins, Preparation H, antiseptic salve, arnica, menstrual sponge, Elastoplast Band-Aids
- several metres of nylon cord
- "leashes" for items loose in the cockpit that might stray or sink in a dump: water bottle, billy, camera bag, binocs. Paddle can be leashed as well. Nylon shock cords with clips either end work well.

IT'S A FINE, STIFF DAY. I drum over the deer trails early to a place where the stream has some depth, where I can worm out over the water on the fallen logs and fill my bottle. We're waiting for the tide and in no hurry. Bob takes us into the woods to look at old trees. These grandfather cedar and spruce grow very straight, not like the ones I saw whirling and bursting into boles on Vancouver Island. The behaviour of trees is a regional thing. Old-growth forest like this is a jumble, trees at every stage of life growing helter-skelter together, an understory of young and a canopy of mature trees mixed in with old, toppled ones that lie on the ground nursing new sprouts, their jagged stumps friable and dramatic.

In the case of second-growth forests there was an event, like lumbering or fire, that levelled everything. All the new growth starts together. The trees are all at the same place in their lives and have a smoother, more symmetrical look. In the old-growth tangle we have here, Bob points to some cedar scars the Haida made stripping off the bark a century or so ago. The light comes through in shimmering blotches, stained green. The forest is very still. Bob loses us after a while and we have to find our own way back.

There's a terrific wind out of Windy Bay, current and wind funnelling in with the tide. When we're clear and turn north, the sea falls slack. There's nothing to brace against in the calm, the mind finds no toehold. To relieve the tedium I recite "The Cremation of Sam McGee" to Bob. We fish a bit and make stops to eat candy.

Mid-afternoon we reach Kunga Island, a looming place with the old village of Tanu a leap across the water. We land on a steep, narrow beach with smooth black pebbles, slim pickings for ground fit to pitch a tent on. We string out along the edge of the trees and spend a silvery evening eyeing Tanu—tomorrow's outing—across the water.

Only days left now and the group is past storming. The outlines around the twosomes have blurred, everyone corralled under the merging force of the trip. Jim from Vegas has never forgiven me for objecting to his cigarette butts early on, but at least, after many days of swimming together and mumbling over welts and bruises, we women are in harmony. I've been reading aloud Haida tales from Anne Cameron's *Daughters of Copper Woman* at campfires the last several nights. The stories are exactly from these beaches. Even Bob parks within earshot.

JULY 12

Big wind this morning, blowing sideways down the water between Kunga and Tanu. I clang my way over the stones to hunch in the intertidal zone, a ritual I like, squatting in my wet shoes looking out to sea. My skin is starting to reject saltwater dousing.

We have a prolonged pancake breakfast propped against drift logs, waiting for the water to steady. Heather crouches over the pan flipping pancakes, her wild hair bundled; Bob, toque pushed back, legs straight out and crossed at the ankles, plays his concertina. When the wind drops, we leave our tents set up on Kunga and cross to Tanu. This is an end-of-trip luxury, two nights in the same camp.

At low tide Tanu beach has ramparts, a ragged buttress of rock cones sticking out of the sea. It was a large settlement, twenty-five to forty houses, facing two directions from a headland. Some five hundred people had to abandon it when smallpox ran through, taking so many lives there were not enough survivors to carry on village life. Now all the poles have fallen or been taken. There's nothing left of the houses but the old foundations, shadows in the ground, their supporting beams toppled into the hollows and furred with moss. The place we visited at the start of the trip, Ninstints on Skun Gwaii, crackled with spirits, but Tanu feels abandoned, long gone, completely neutral.

The forest Emily Carr painted pushes into the village from behind, the spruce and hemlock very straight, their roots like bird claws grasping huge clumps of earth mounded ten, fifteen feet high. The canopy makes a pagan church, tree trunks careening to heaven.

We wander by ourselves. I find a burying place, a quiet lawn of low trees with one broken headstone bearing an engraving of a ruffled English sleeve in a handshake. It looks odd in this pagan place, this envoy, like a cluster of Christian spores flung out from Europe, landing meaninglessly, mouldering away without any link to its host.

The cove beyond is a hodgepodge of driftwood, and I spend a long time picking it over, thinking about the Haida and about Leon. I'm out of all sense of what anyone at home would make of this, or how to tell them.

JULY 13

Last day. We make a dash four miles down Tanu, sailing our reefed boats to the pickup point where the plane will fetch us tomorrow. For me it is poignant. I don't know when I'll paddle again or if I'll ever find my way into these islands again. Bob and I trade appreciation. He is specific. He commends me on my steady paddling and sensitivity to the place, and thanks me for asking so little of him.

We have an east-facing beach at our last camp, the hills hunkered behind in dark conference. We soon lose the sun. Shadows spread into the ocean and I move from point to point to stay in the light. Wedged out of the wind, I write a letter to Bree, rinse a few things, anchor them to dry, and think about what I'll need for the trip up the panhandle. I'm in a limbo state, the senses hanging on, unslakeable, the brain gone on. Dinner and evening are solemn in deep shade. The sun goes down without a murmur.

JULY 14

This morning we're picking at peanut butter and jam, waiting for the plane in damp shoes, calm and wistful and relieved.

Five

THE INSIDE PASSAGE

S outheast Alaska is an outer ruffle of the broad cordillera that stretches along the coast of North America, from California north to the Alaska Peninsula, that skeletal foot into the Pacific Ocean where it meets the Bering Sea. This landform is the work of tectonic action between continental and Pacific plates. Fifty or sixty million years ago the geological scum that we know as North America began drifting its way northwest, crunching and grinding into collision with a young sea floor, shoving the continent into stony puckers five thousand feet high.

On a topographical map you can see the run of fjords, the state of rumpled uplift at the edge of this event. The cliffs indicate the fault line, the weak collision between two geologic plates. Glacial ice twelve thousand years ago scoured out the crumbling and broken rock from these fault zones and left them as flooded valleys, the bony-fingered, drizzling fjords known as the Inside Passage.

JULY 19

Signal Creek is a small campground in a rain forest five miles north of Ketchikan, Alaska, out of reach of the stench of the town's pulp and paper mill. I ride here on my bicycle from the ferry docks, my load so imbalanced I'm afraid the front wheel is going to rear up and throw me. Now that this leg of the journey is upon me, I wish I'd thought it through. My bicycle is a mélange of spare parts; I barely used it on the gravel roads around the schoolhouse, and we're not acquainted yet. The problems are fairly evident. I need to distribute the load front and back so I don't have fifty pounds of weight on my rear wheel and virtually nothing on the front. I need fat tires with thick treads for these gravel roads, not skittish racing tires. I'm in the mountains; I need more than one gear. Where are the other nine on this thing?

I labour my way to camp in a blast of afternoon heat, trying to decant as much weight as possible through my arms into the handlebars. On the grades I have to get off and push the whole wobbly assemblage ahead of me.

An unencumbered cyclist who introduces himself as John, from Wyoming, joins me partway along, remarking on the obvious. He offers to bring an order catalogue around later, presumably so I can outfit myself with a front rack. There are a lot of men in Alaska. In summer they outnumber women five to one, filling

up the coast to work the salmon boats. If my incompetence continues, I could become a beacon in the area.

I choose a huge campsite in an arbour of giant Sitkas near the
camp entrance. The trees give immediate solace, like grandmothers,
and I sit down in their midst. This is the improvisational part of the
trip that's been hard to picture. I have about a month to make my
way up the B.C. coast to the Yukon before I'm due back south in the
Gulf Islands for a ten-day yoga residential I signed up for last spring.
A month is a short time to visit a huge place, but a long time to pitch
a tent on strange ground every night. I don't know how it'll go.

Travelling the ferries is fun. The one I took out of Prince
Rupert this morning was like a huge rumbling wedding cake. It had
several decks, the best of them equipped with a see-through plastic
awning where passengers can get out of the rain. Some backpackers were staking out floor space when I made a tour. I found powerful showers in several never-to-be-found-again locations and fresh
berry pie in the cafeteria. I spent the trip in a deck chair perusing
the ferry schedule, the sky so blue it seemed shocked. Arrivals and
departures are set by the tides, not by human convenience, and
about half the dockings I scanned occur in the middle of the night
or are listed as "approximate," since tides follow the moon.

This shuttle, the Alaska Marine Highway, runs between Seattle
and Prince Rupert at its southern terminus, up the Alaska panhandle
to Skagway in the north. The route is a 700-kilometre slither

through the protected islands scattered along the coast. The ferries stop at about a dozen fishing and lumber communities along the way, all of them, past Rupert, inaccessible by land except Haines and Skagway. At both these towns there are historical routes inland over the mountains to the Yukon or the Alaska Highway. The ferry trip between Rupert and Skagway takes about thirty-two hours if you don't stop over anywhere, not counting the detour some runs make to Sitka on the outer coast. If you debark along the way, you can catch the next ferry whenever you like; they run like buses. Taking a car on board is expensive and requires reservations, but if you walk on, with a kayak or bicycle, you need only show up and pay your fare. It's a well-loved mode of travel for its informality. Common practice is to sleep on the solarium deck anywhere there's space to unroll a sleeping bag. Chaise longues are available, and the idea is to snag one as fast as you can get upstairs when you board.

A TRAIL LOOPS over the creek that runs through the campground, and I drum along it after supper, the chortle of ravens and the screech of a young eagle ricocheting through the trees. I recognize Sitka spruce by the purple sheen on the bark, and salal in low, glossy bundles along the path. It is drier here than on Haida Gwaii, the sky sharp and high and the ground a scuffle of duff. There's a feast of berries on the bushes: pale orange soapberries like inflated raspberries, gooseberries, redcurrants.

A sign on the trail calls this a "climax" forest—vegetation grow-ing under the best possible conditions. I've come during salmon harvest, the season when the fish, sleek from living in the ocean, return to their birthing rivers to spawn. On the way they'll turn colour, go from silver to Day-Glo rose or rusty green. I've seen them in the spawning beds after their ordeal, an air of surfeit about them, their heads battered and snaggle-toothed, their bodies haggard.

JULY 20

I'm on a tree stump in my campsite this morning, the com-pany of spruce around me exuding an air of kindness with their ancient trunks and quiet limbs and drizzle of dusty needles. They soar up to some other stratum, imperceptible from the ground, where they're young and gleaming and growing fast in the light.

Their atmosphere makes me want to stay around, but I coax my bike out into the dazzling road with half my gear and coast back to the ferry docks to stow my load in a locker—a manoeuvre meant to spare me a repeat of yesterday when I leave. I wrap my bicycle seat in my toque to re-contour it. There's no relation what-soever between the human pelvis and the design of bicycle seats.

Now that the gold is gone, Ketchikan gets by on salmon can-neries, sawmills and tourism. There are two huge cruise ships in town at the moment, in a sweltering heat wave. Ketchikan's motto is, "If it isn't raining in Ketchikan, wait five minutes," and the citizens look unnerved by this climatic mutiny. I walk my bike around town, peeling off layers of clothes. The streets are jammed with shoppers. Every store has the same enticements, the same real-fur toy seals on key rings, the same sliding silver buckles on leather lariats, the same miniature totem poles and decorated fur moccasins.

I head out of the hub and watch some Native kids leaping off the bridge into Ketchikan Creek, limbs untidy and exuberant. The salmon hatchery, further on, has no tourists. It's a group of low buildings in shade, linked by interpretive signs that explain the life cycle of the coho or "king" salmon. In the last building there are pools, fake homelands, containing millions of shimmering finger-lings being raised for release into the ocean. I follow along, stunned by these astounding fish and their kamikaze swim. Does fostering them here mean they'll have to hurl themselves on the hatchery lawn when it's time to spawn?

I heard about a large totem park a few miles out of town and, with the heat abating, I churn out along the shore road to look. On a slope of parched grass facing the sea I find the poles, painted house-paint colours, carved in a crude, cartoonish way. They must be a spoof. Someone must have thought the vaunted Haida poles were too serious and needed parody. These posts, so I hear, are transplants from their original villages, but they have no artistry or verve at all. I don't know why they're here.

I sit in the grass watching the flat shapes of shore and water, almost invisible in the late white sun. I'm miserable and can't figure out why. Everything I see looks like those tawdry poles.

Back in town just at closing time, I get a chocolate malt in a filmed aluminum shaker almost too cold to touch. There's no one in the café and it's refreshingly dim. The waitress is middle-aged, in a rumpled shirtwaist and nurse shoes. She chats while she swabs the floors, telling me she intends to leave Ketchikan sometime and go visit her son in Montana. "You get feeling trapped any place you're in," she says.

JULY 21

A lost chance last night, which I regretted all day. John whatever-his-name-is, from Wyoming, who walked me into camp the other day, came by last night with a bike catalogue. I'd already gone to bed and it spooked me to hear my name called in a place where I'm a stranger. I couldn't recover myself to crawl out and visit with him, and after a while I guess he rode the six miles back to town. I thought about trying to find the boat he's seining on, but I don't know what it's called.

Six weeks from home, I'm longing for company. I get in small chats in grocery stores or campgrounds, but mostly I travel as though encased in Plexiglas. Crossing the country was a pleasure. Solitude was new terrain—like swimming underwater with a breathing hose—

but I don't think prolonging my isolation on the kayaking trip added to a good thing. Being alone in a group isn't solitude, it's lack of connection. Ultimately wearing.

This guy from Wyoming was friendly, and after fifteen days in the Charlottes paddling incommunicado, an unrestrained gab with anybody would have been a relief.

I wheel my bike onto the ferry this afternoon in a funk. The *Malaspina* has a vast storage belly and more decks than seems safe. In my present state no one on board looks like anyone I want to talk to, except for one ropy, white-haired woman on her own, with her sleeves rolled up over her elbows and very brown knuckles. She approaches me this evening and introduces herself as Audrey Sutherland, on her way to Juneau to paddle for the summer, her habit for the past twelve years. She lives in Hawaii and writes books about kayaking. She's sixty-three.

"You're pretty intrepid, paddling alone all summer."

"Why not?" she says. "No one knows how fast I go."

She gives me her address and takes my picture on the doused black wharf at Wrangell when I get off with my bike at midnight.

I speed along a battered, empty road to a baseball diamond where camping's allowed, and put up my tent by feel in the inky dark. Just as I crawl in, I hear a van or some kind of truck pull into the park and come to a halt ten feet from me. Some locals and their dates, several sheets to the wind, settle in for the after-hours leg of the evening. I worm to the back of the tent, praying for cover of darkness. I don't want an encounter in a strange town in the middle of the night. Either they can't see me or the sight of a nylon hump out the truck window is unexceptional; nobody bothers me. While beer bottles thunk around the tent, I eavesdrop on a long, unimaginative excoriation of Wrangell citizenry. When they drive off at last, I get out of the tent and, irrationally, move it.

JULY 22

This morning the world looks sharp-edged and brilliant, like after a heart attack, every detail adrenalin-scoured. I see I'm in a cemetery, not a ball field, and I'm not alone. There are two backpackers fast asleep on a picnic table the next lot over. Where were they during the hijinks?

There's a ferry at noon and I don't plan to stay around Wrangell. Riding out on my bike, the town looks frowzy and played out. I pass rusted-out car parts in untended yards, heaved sidewalks fringed with crabgrass, lanky wildflowers humpbacked in the ditches. A despondent sign, drooping on its fittings, announces, "Open Some Afternoons." I hurry on, as if slowing to look would be unkind.

There's time before the ferry to hunt on the beach for the petroglyphs Audrey told me about. The rock here has a creased, soft look, like Plasticine. After a while I find them, worn spiral shapes and blocky human faces with bull's eyes, depressions in the stone that seem pressed by some ancient finger, strangely stirring. While I stand in the clutter of rock, the bright green tide dashes in, filling the shore in minutes as if a huge gate on the horizon had been lifted.

EVERY BOAT is more monstrous than the last. Could the *Columbia* be even bigger than the leviathan I was on yesterday? I can't figure out what's wrong with me. Another grand funk. Am I bad at being in motion? I've felt homeless and itchy since Ketchikan.

I conclude it's Haida Gwaii hangover, too fast a toppling from the heady air of those old camps and beaches to these clanging boat decks. The border between the nerves and the world is only skin, after all. We hurl ourselves from place to place, but really we don't transpose so easily.

And the boats wear me out.

I like being alone when there's no one around. It's a nice free-dom to be the only one there, humming and coping, following my impulse. Being by myself in a public place is different, though, and requires a certain sturdiness. It brings in the element of self-consciousness. I'm not past wondering how I appear to others, gear-encumbered and obviously on a journey of some length. I don't look like a woman hopping up the channel to the next town to watch her son play baseball. Do people think I couldn't get anyone to come with me? Maybe I look like I'm impossible to live with.

In the long run it's probably easier, causes less wear and tear, to be with somebody. On the boats I notice most people are. They're preoccupied in families or couples, and don't have to think about what to do while visible to strangers. The usual dodge for loners is to read or make journal entries or watch scenery intently, but that's a giveaway. The mark of a person travelling alone is to look resolute.

IN LATE, BRIGHT afternoon, we churn in to Petersburg, a Tyrolean village strung along the shore. Many lacquered shutters with cut-out hearts welcome the traveller, though not the camper: there is nowhere to pitch a tent.

At last I scrounge a few feet in someone's yard and think about leaving as soon as possible, my response to all these towns.

In the laundromat, a fellow from California says there's nothing to do around here but drink. Given he's about twenty years old, I'm surprised he sees this as a drawback. He tells me he's here can-ning salmon roe for the Japanese and can't wait to take his five thousand dollars and go home.

JULY 23

Last night I dreamt about friends. We'd all been in Haida Gwaii or somewhere preternatural. An old lover had been doing some kind of work that discoloured his arms; they were blue as a tattoo. The trend of these dreams is always the same: I cannot quite find my place, I want to be closer in but can't.

I had a pleasant walk around the wharf after dinner, the water shining and languid at sundown and the pilings long. Timbered hills pen the town, and beyond them the crumpled mountains along the horizon flared pink. Norwegian decals on all the houses are something to overcome, but the gardens and waysides brim with nasturtiums, calendula and forget-me-nots, like a vote for anarchy.

In this town, fishing proceeds year-round. Petersburg's one street has a look of prosperity, two-storey frame buildings freshly painted and set tidily side by side. Today I have breakfast in a café at six-thirty, catching the men before they go out on their boats. Across the gender chasm I get into a conversation with a fisherman in his sixties, who tells me what he thinks about government regulations on fishing and forestry.

"I hate these new rules. They've put a halt on roadwork and logging over in Sitka till they figure out who owns the land. A piece of stupidity because of a bunch of people in San Francisco who've never even been to Sitka, or anywhere up here. I don't like meddling and I hate land claims settlements and I'll tell you why. When Indians go to court and get it settled that they own the land, they don't have to follow the same rules other loggers abide by— regulations on board feet, say. They're free to clear-cut their trees, and they damn well do. This notion about understanding the land is bunk. Indians saw down their trees same as anyone else, and then they go to court for more land. I liked their granddaddies fine, but these here ones are not the same at all."

These are fighting words, but the anguish in his face stops me cold. When I leave, a bumper sticker on a pickup outside reads, "Make jobs, not wilderness."

I guess we want things simple.

JULY 24

Audrey's address bit it this morning when I used the napkin she wrote on to mop up a spill in my tent. My connections here are so frail, I'm sorry to lose this one.

I give up on a mountain hike, worried about bears, and settle for a cycle around town, during which I find some lower gears, my ten-speed behaving like a ten-speed after all. I spend the afternoon in a dried-up bog, reading and looking up every few minutes, sipping the view. Yellow grass and scabby lodgepole pine fan out in the distance, making their way to dark spruce, the trees spreading over black foothills and up at last to a crinoline of snow mountains where the sky fits the land.

I'm reading natural history, how mountains form soil. It did not occur to me that they do, that mountains are in motion. The force of ice and erosion works away down through millennia, breaking off bits of rock, shoving it downward off the mountains, grinding it finer and finer, pushing it into the lowlands, making soil, in an action that never ceases.

Landscape, which looks so constant, is on the move. The mountains dream on the horizon, but mountains are just passing through. I watch them, wearing, grinding, rising up out there, their motion still the main beat.

JULY 25

The night I left Petersburg, the weather changed. I felt it on the ferry, the wind gusting around my deck chair, nosing into my sleeping bag. I had to get up and move under the solarium. Now the aberrant dry is gone; it's back to rainy business.

This is Sitka, first a Tlingit, then a Russian, now an American port, on the frayed outer edge of the coast. After some hunting I get a good campsite around the bay from the ferry dock, a den where the trees spread low, all hollows and alcoves, with a natural table where a limb sprawls sideways.

The town is draped along the shore a few miles down, and when I've got my camp organized I ride out. A supermarket I pass along the way stocks fresh orange juice and pesto and stays open till eleven every night. These towns may be mountain-locked, but they're American through and through.

Sitka has a compact centre with a long stretch of park around the beach. The Tlingit and Russian heritage leans forward on every street to catch tourists. I ride around in fine rain, get my bike adjusted, buy a tiny argillite carving for Leon. When it starts raining hard, I take cover in the museum, in the wild lost lives salvaged there, the artifacts of the Northwest tribes—Aleut, Athapaskan, Tlingit, Tsimshan and Haida.

It's a dusky place, grey light coming through windows high in the walls, the planed floor set with old glass cases like cupboards, the objects inside faint and melancholy. The collection is arranged chronologically. Remnants of a thousand years' culture work up to the arrival of the Europeans, the new tools and materials the foreigners brought comically and intricately absorbed into the old designs: carved top hats adorning warriors, teacups made of grass. Chilkats went mad on beadwork, stitching bits of European glass into their ceremonial bibs and leggings. The Aleut made exquisite baskets, twined impossibly tight and embellished with tiny designs, vestiges of an interim trading time when the two cultures, European and Native, benefited alike.

In dull glass cases are some Athapaskan garments made of moose and caribou hides. These inland forest people left the fur on the skin, turning it inward against their bodies in winter. The skins were tanned in an animal-brain solution and smoked to the colour of pollen.

In another case are Inuit clothes: tailored parkas of skin, fur and translucent gut, footwear lined with dried grass, woven grass socks to fit inside boots. They used the intestines of sea mammals or fish skins to make opaque Early Gore-Tex garments, waterproof and windproof. We think insulation, convection and wicking away moisture are new-tech, but the Inuit knew all about staying warm and dry.

Their wooden masks were planed smooth and painted a limpid white, with simple cut-outs for eyes and mouth. They look like thin ghosts sprouting scrawny and comical feathers from their heads. There are finger masks and carved rings with tiny antic faces mounted on them.

Inuit hunting weapons were ivory, fantastically carved. I see one with a procession of caribou half an inch high trailing over the arc of a bow. Another has inlaid figures, spidery and delicate in the yellowing bone. The everyday objects of these people's lives were works of art—cooking baskets, tools, weapons raised far beyond function.

The Russians came to Sitka in the eighteenth century to hunt sea otter to decorate the czars. Swatches of the pelts of a dozen fur-bearing animals are displayed, showcasing the beauty of the sea otter's dense and sparkling fur, superior even to mink. The Russians called the pelts "soft gold" and hunted sea otter to the brink of extinction.

WHEN THE RAIN subsides I reel outside, where the story continues, history portrayed on a two-mile loop through the rain forest. There are Haida totems in the park, brought here in 1939 and reconstructed by local carvers. They show fine craftsmanship, but for me the new paint severs the link with the past.

Sitka was Tlingit. When the Tlingit got in the way of the Russians' full-bore plunder of sea otter, they were driven out of Shee Atika, their ancestral village. The story goes that the Tlingit came back a generation later and rebuilt their homes outside the Russian barracks. Along the path there are bleached paintings showing the burning of the Russian fort, Redoubt, by Tlingit in 1802 and the retaliation of a thousand Russian soldiers in 1804. One painting shows Katlian, a Tlingit warrior, his hammer raised in a Mel Gibson arm, his head stuck in a helmet like a bucket, bearing down on a dozen armed Russians in Buster Brown sailor hats, who stagger back in dismay. The courage of these stumpy men astounds me, chanting and fasting and paddling their war boats hundreds of miles in the open ocean, attacking halibut and enemies with their toothed clubs. They are always depicted as ferocious, yet what strikes me is their fear. Why else chant and fast but to ward off abject terror?

I read the following account:

When the Russians returned with their navy, the Tlingit entered the stockade where ships' cannon pounded for six days. The night of the sixth day, Russians heard chanting from within the stockade. At dawn, flocks of raven were hovering over the fort. Within the abandoned walls,

Russians found dried fish and provisions for over seven hundred inhabitants and the bodies of dead children. The Tlingit had disappeared into the forest. After burning the fort to the ground, the Russians looted and burned Shee Atika. On the ashes of the village, they built the stockade settlement of New Archangel—the forerunner of Sitka.

So much for the Tlingit.

It's the old story I remember from grade school, the meaning incomprehensible to a nine-year-old. History had a different interpretation then. It was more a football scrimmage, nature and Indians on the one side, pernicious and anonymous, and white Europeans, persevering and destined, on the other.

Being on site like this has peculiar force. In the rain and dark trees, the drab ocean flopping beside me, I catch the way it must have gone: The Russian presence, not large but long-standing, the fur trade proceeding with the Tlingit in a bearable way, gradually heating up as the demand in Russia grows and the Tlingit commit themselves more and more to trapping. But the Indians content to have it grow, thriving, paddling out in their boats to meet the ships, relishing an interlude of fair trade, a rise above subsistence. Then some competitive poking around from the English and Spanish, more ships abroad, more pressure. Still the liaison holding. More village labour goes to trapping, the balance kept but doomed. More and more Europeans in the New World, more people than the Indians have ever seen. Then the real cash crop is found: "soft gold" on the bodies of sea otter. Sea otter fur booms among the Russian aristocracy, a fashion must. The demand swamps the villages. The Russians don't want middlemen any more, find it more expeditious to hunt sea otter themselves. They know how; they've been in the region for years. So they hunt sea otter almost to extinction. They take them all.

I make my way along, coming out of the hoop of history like waking up, and all at once I'm fed up and weary, as though I've been in the woods forever—the weight of these trees, the whirling salal bushes, the hiss of shore water on small stones, the forever burbling and commentary of raven, bundled close and smothering under the sodden sky. I've attended so closely to these grey beaches, had so little relief, it's as though there's no difference between us. My forehead is the drizzling air, my eyeballs the wet trees, the pads on my fingers the round beach stones.

JULY 26

The trip's half over. Home is a distant town, the tracts of country between here and there too huge for home to seem real. Overall my mood is glum, but in one respect I'm at a good stage. I'm getting the hang of this. I've worked out the bugs of camping on and off the ferry. When I started I seemed to spend about half my time looking for the grommets on the tarp with rain running down my neck. Now I've sped it up a bit, got it going smoother. I can find the shower on the boat reliably, I'm down to the five items of clothing I really use, I've located all the gears on my bike. A bit of know-how makes me grin from ear to ear. I don't take competence for granted. Everything in the life of a ferry-hopping cyclist is a feat: reconnoitring; finding a flat, drained, protected, hospitable, bear-free, legal spot every night for the tent; getting oriented fast so I can explore and have some fun; then packing up and doing it all over again in the next place.

I know women can do it. There are woodswomen all over the place. Probably these physical skills are matter-of-fact to a great many of them, but to me they're completely alluring, the *crème de la crème.* Nothing I've done matches the pleasure, the pure exuberance of these small occasions when I can get it all going, when I'm out of doors, comfortable and dry, stuffing my senses. Despite a late start I expect to spend the rest of my life dashing off the highway, pursuing this know-how, plumbing the outdoors side of life. I expect to be a little old solo woman with outdoors acumen, poking around with tarps and knots and fussy camp stoves somewhere out of range.

JULY 27

I've been looking forward to Juneau, to the thrill of docking at four in the morning in this big panhandle town that got to be state capital, a gold-mining settlement wedged between two mountains.

Because the channel's clogged with glacial sediment, the ferry docks fourteen miles north of town.

It's daylight when I get off, water and sky the colour of cold silver. I call my parents, and my father, eating breakfast in Ontario, says, "Come home. All is forgiven."

I pedal to a campsite described in my guidebook as impressively close to Mendenhall Glacier and put up my tent in a thicket of willows beside the speeding runoff. I mean to crawl in and sleep, but the riled, probing cold off the water is unnerving. I see the glacier beyond, a dirty blue sponge clamped to the base of the mountains. Chill envelops the campground, the water in the taps iron-tasting, the ground sooty. There's a gloomy, ill-natured damp to the place, and I wonder if the glacier is to blame.

I leave my tent and ride away to scout.

The U.S. Forest Service has built a handsome visitor centre at the edge of the glacier, equipped with decks and telescopes and lofty windows, and at nine a.m. tourists in head scarves and mitts are milling around, beating their arms to keep warm.

Flanking the glacier on either side are ribbons of vegetation that show the history of its retreat. The swath of most recent withdrawal is stripped to bare gravel, but the next ribbon shows fireweed and lupine taking hold. The lesson on "Succession" in the visitor centre explains that fireweed is the emblem of the north, showing up in abundance after any assault. You see it washing the mountains in summer, its blowy purple spires dabbing the gash of clear-cut or fire. It is always the first growth in a recovery, and when it withers, it provides morsels of earth and nitrogen to root the next wave of vegetation, alder and willow. These shrubs flank the glacier we're staring at, straying thinly down the slope. In a hundred years, or three hundred, their leaves will make enough compost for soft-woods, Sitka spruce and hemlock.

Riding away from the glacier, I see tourists clumped at the side of the road, their attention taken by something. In a pool where the creek eddies, salmon are resting on their run. They swim slowly, their bodies bulging with eggs, their skin the intense vermilion of exalted effort.

JUNEAU IS LIKE A SPIDER. The sheer mountains make it impossible for the centre to enlarge, so the town sends out thin legs of habitation into the Mendenhall Valley and along the shore. The glacier at the head of the valley is now a Juneau suburb, complete with a bus stop. Downtown hangs on a mountainside seven or eight streets high, the climb from the waterfront nearly vertical. People mounting the streets have to bend in half or tack. It's a gold rush town, and at the moment it's full of cheerful tourists having cappuccinos. I have one too and then go visit Inuit technology in the state museum, scribbling tiny notes and trying to pin what I see to the backs of my eyeballs forever.

There are snow goggles—a slit in a deer antler, worn mounted on the nose; a gut parka decorated with lateral rows of curling bird feathers, each feather held in place by a tiny clamped beak; an umiak—an Aleut open boat—the frame made of driftwood, held together with hide lashing and pegs and covered in walrus hide, tough and waterproof, built for hunting large sea mammals, walrus and whale. Contrary to popular belief, the Inuit did not roll in their boats; the term "Eskimo roll" is probably a misnomer. The first sea kayakers carried floaters—the inflated stomachs of seals—to give their boats ballast in the ocean and to act as markers of animals taken.

There are dance mitts covered in puffin beaks, a belt of caribou teeth set close like pearls, gums overlapping. There is a 2000-year-old ivory sculpture—a phallus with a female head, the face simple and magical, the mouth a slit without lips, the nose long and solemn, the eyes hooded. I see reversible coats again, one made of skin from the breasts of cormorants, murres, auklets, puffins, loons and geese, worn with feathers out in wet weather or turned inward in the dry and cold. This dress is decorated with dyed porcupine quills, shells, dried berries, feathers and fur. Glass beads came later.

The ingenuity astounds me. How did they devise these curing baths of urine, caribou brains, water and roe? How did they know a smoky fire and hours of scraping would turn the hide to cream?

JULY 28

More rain. I dash into town and eat breakfast in a homesick coffee shop that reminds me of Queen Street in Toronto, the waitress presiding in shorts and T-shirt. She fries up blueberry pecan pancakes on the grill and entertains her customers with local baseball news. Baseball teams in the panhandle use the ferry to get to their games.

The Harbor Washboard, next on the chore list, is the best laundromat I've ever seen. Twenty-foot ceilings keep the air airlike, a shower token buys an unlimited burst of strong, hot spray, and a two-dollar deposit gets you a fragrant, worn towel and a washcloth. By the dryers an Asian grandmother tries to keep a rein on two toddlers, but gives up and lets them run around, slamming themselves against the warm machines.

No rules are posted in the laundromat, just the hours they're open and an apology for no change. Aerial photographs of Juneau curl on the walls. Two rows of plastic chairs, smoking and nonsmoking, are set congenially side by side.

All my clothes are in the wash and I sit naked in my rain gear, reading an old *New Yorker*. This is truly time out. For the time being I do not live in a tent on a freezing riverbank.

When the rain stops, the weather promptly turns muggy and buggy. I re-attire myself, take my bicycle downtown, park it outside a bookstore and start toiling up the hill, bent double, to take a walk in the mountains.

On the trail it takes a long time to get used to the sticky air and the coating of flies clinging to my arms and hair, and to surmount the ambivalence I have about hiking alone. But I've noticed this about leaving town: there comes a point when whatever zone of habitation you came from fades out and the venture opens up. The land spreads out, sparkling, and the sensation is mostly sound, a slight electric hum that you feel in your solar plexus, thrilling and quieting both.

The hills are steep, stroked in alder and spruce, which means the vegetation's not very advanced. The land here must slide so often that the trees have to keep starting over. There are pale green bands running down the slopes, slowly filling the slide paths. The watery air makes the view glimmer. The mountainsides are tickled by thin, fast-falling rivers spreading like veins in an old hand from small, clean-cut dabs of snow in the hollows of the peaks.

A FUNNY THING happens in the bookstore later. When I'm ready to leave, a title catches my eye: *Paddling My Own Canoe* by a Hawaiian paddler, writing up her kayaking adventures. I recognize the name of the author from the defunct napkin. Audrey Sutherland, lost and found.

I GET INTO A CONVERSATION with a man and woman in a gold rush bar. He is a voluble, commanding person with a wide, rippling white beard; she, years younger and rather quiet. Perhaps she's heard his stories too many times, but she's diplomatic and relaxed and we pass a pleasant time. He's well travelled, a connoisseur of Native art, which leads us to the Haida. He checks my effusiveness.

"They weren't angels, you know. They had a stratified society—slaves and aristocracy. Those poles were built on cheap labour, same as the pyramids."

He says if I'm going further north I must go to Atlin, back of the coast in the mountains of British Columbia. This is the second time someone's told me Atlin is the most beautiful place on earth. Bonnie, who ran the bed and breakfast on Sandspit, said she's moving there as soon as the Charlottes are ruined. The anticipation of dry air comes as such a relief, it's as though I've been holding my breath. When I look at my map later, I see I can get off the coast and over the mountains at Haines—next stop.

JULY 29

Haines, Alaska, is the homeland of the Chilkat, a proud, wealthy people famous among the coastal tribes for their woven blankets. They could get anything they wanted in barter for the gold and blue work of these capes. Their village is now a spacious town on a broad swerve of shore, the streets and buildings laid out roomily in front of vaulting mountains. The mountains I take on faith, since it's drizzling when I steer my bike off the ferry, the sky drooped about twenty feet above the road.

Haines, unlike all the other panhandle towns except Skagway, is connected to the interior by road, an old trade route that follows the Chilkat River through the mountains. During the Second World War the route was upgraded to a paved road to connect with the under-construction Alaska Highway. As I ride into town, the sense of greater access is palpable. The place draws overland visitors from Tok and Anchorage as well as people off the cruise ships. I pass a formidable number of gift and craft shops downtown. A bunch of ten-year-olds are standing outside a forty-six-flavour ice cream parlour smoking and shoving each other.

Looking for a campground, I find the Chilkat heritage curiously represented on a hillside south of the town. The historical site of Fort Seward is on a broad, treeless slope sweeping up from the sea. The perimeter of the lawn is set with tidy English frame buildings, resembling garden sheds, their symmetry at odds with the soaring disorder of mountains behind. In the centre of the lawn, encircled by the English buildings, is a Chilkat lodge, brand new, built in the traditional style, with carved house posts facing the sea and painted dark coral, turquoise and black. I wonder if building the lodge surrounded by English buildings is intended to be symbolic.

Despite the eclipse of Native culture in all these towns—or so it seems—Chilkat ancestry at Haines is visible in the land itself, in the choice of site. Scrape off the town and you see the way the natural protection of the cove would have set the original village at a good advantage in war and hemmed it against the wind. The river into the mountains provides passage to the interior and a supply of fish and game. The middens remain, hollows on the beach full of shellfish bones, remnants of summer meals. From the woods comes the creaking cry of Chilkat descendants, great-grandchildren eagles gliding from perch to perch.

I FIND A CAMPGROUND past Fort Seward, a drenched triangle of grass above the shore. My tent is soaked by the time I get it up. It's in my mind that in a day or so I'm off the coast, out of this rain and over the mountains, and as usual when change is coming, I don't want to go.

I dip into town life tonight in the Bamboo Room restaurant. It's shaped like a boxcar with Naugahyde banquettes down two sides, Formica tables and astonishing views of the mountains. There aren't more than a dozen tables, all of them full. I notice that no one is conversing. People sit alone or in morose groups, eating. There's a family of five in the corner, all the children very small. Every time the baby cries, the father looks down at the floor. A man with long bony thighs sitting by himself across from me is reading a manual beside a meal that appears to be six muffins covered in an inch of sour cream. A woman in sweatpants and earrings dithers over the menu, asks for spaghetti, leaves the restaurant for about ten minutes, and returns having added a black wool toque and dinner rings. A rumpled woman with huge, yellowing hazel eyes sits down next to me and begins a dialogue with the waitress.

"What vegetables do you have?"

"Carrots."

"Again?"

She asks the waitress for a side order of mushrooms.

"Canned or fresh?"

"What's the difference?"

"Well, one comes from a can and the other's fresh."

"Canned. And an order of carrots and a small french fries."

Later on, this woman is joined by Ray, with whom she shares her fries. Ray puts them in a Styrofoam cup. "I'll heat them later," he says.

I begin talking with them and Ray tells me about the greatest Canadian cowboy, Lorne Greene.

JULY 30

The wind shifted this afternoon, chasing the rain out of the channel. I sat on the shore and watched the barricade of clouds that blocked the view thin and creep away up the mountains, unveiling timber, bald rock and snow. The shore across the water is quite close, the channel blowing aquamarine spray. On my beach stones, fireweed and scrawny spruce lie about higgledy-piggledy, as if dropped from an airplane. There are some comely boat wrecks in back of the beach, and a bunch of ravens overhead are bellyaching in the wind.

I have a perfect dinner: macaroni alfredo on my tiny camp stove, served with screw-top white wine. Out over the fireweed two hummingbirds joust in mid-air. The water is grey-green silk, the colour of bay leaves. The wind has dropped and there are no bugs. Mountains across the way are banded in light and shadow, and in the shade the timber looks like animal fur, plush and dark. Against the dark, the lit snow gleams in geographic shapes—England and Africa. A skirt of cloud, edges wafting and dissolving, floats up.

JULY 31

I've stowed my bike in a back room at the ferry dock. In the Yukon the distances will be too great to use a bike. I'll pick it up on the way back. I'm down to a backpack with camping gear and one change of underwear.

I leave Haines on the 6 a.m. bus bound for Haines Junction in the Yukon. The driver is garrulous and regales the dozen or so of us on his run with facts and folklore. "Now this is how fireweed got its name: You see how this plant goes through its cycle. The purple flowers open bottom to top through summer. When they start to die, the leaves turn red—'blaze' you could say—and the end of the stalk looks like a wisp of smoke. Just before the snow, it goes off like a puff."

As the bus climbs, he explains an upcoming phenomenon: alpine tundra in the Haines Pass. "We shouldn't have alpine conditions at this latitude, it's too low. By alpine I mean, no trees. We're above the treeline in the pass at 3,500 feet. Normally you need 12,000 feet to get alpine conditions. And the reason we get it here is the earth's tilt. In these northern latitudes like we have in Alaska, we get conditions you normally don't see." (The Haines Pass is actually in British Columbia, but Americans generally ignore this detail.)

The sober drama of the coast falls behind us. Within an hour of leaving we're well above sea level and blessedly dry. Dust from the road gently sifts up through the floor onto our laps and sandwiches while the driver exhorts us to look out the window. The land is bald. We pass over a high plain where even black spruce have faltered. In the roll of rock and lichen there is only a scribble of alder shrub. The colours are achingly subtle—a precious slipcover laid over the land, worn to silver, green and grey, all wavering tawny pale. The hills bounding the plain have been rubbed smooth and blunt, their bare sides soaking the warmth of the sun like old faces. In some places the rock is rose-gold where some patient lichen has been crawling over the stone for centuries. Some of the hills are stippled by thin waterfalls.

At the height of the pass the driver stops and we tumble out—a group now, bonded by this naked plain, by the amphitheatre of sky, a dry wind coming almost soundless from the edge of the world.

Soon afterwards, back on the bus, we drop under the treeline again and chug over an invisible line into the Yukon. The hand of wind erosion in the pass behind us was old, but these Kluane peaks rip youthfully at the sky, their sides pure grey. This is the lower end of the St. Elias range, the driver drones, containing the San Andreas Fault and many volcanoes.

When the bus drops us in Haines Junction, it's summer, the air warm and piney. My clothes are instantly a burden. I could weep. How long have I been in the damp? The Kluane Park office is here, located at the foot of the mountains. While we wait for the bus to Whitehorse, we watch a slide presentation in the Visitor Centre. Kluane and the American Wrangell–St. Elias Mountains are UNESCO World Heritage Sites, their heart a vast icefield, the largest on earth but for the poles. I've entered an entirely different ecosystem, this land in rain shadow behind the mountains. The soil is cold and gritty, containing little humus. The broad-leafed trees are limited to birch and trembling aspen. The pine and spruce are stunted. *Plants of Northern British Columbia*, a book I peruse after the slide presentation, says tersely, "Only those trees capable of tolerating extended periods of frozen ground occur."

The region is as unlike Central Ontario as the coast I've just escaped, but, standing in the parking lot in warm, dry air, squinting at Kluane's icy peaks, I think, now I'm really here. This is what I came for.

Six

WHITEHORSE

AUGUST 3

My third day in Whitehorse, and from the minute the bus pulled in it's been easy to be here. The restlessness that dogged me on the coast is gone. I slid under the weight of those drowning trees.

The Yukon is sere, the air thin and dry like the best fall days at home. There's frost in the mornings—my fingers ache setting up my stove for tea—but soon the sun heats the air and bakes it all day long. The campground's full of the scent of little pines that are very old and don't grow tall. In the Yukon I sleep long, like an unwinding.

I like the town—or city, rather—four downtown streets, laid out along the Yukon River, trailing into suburbs in the valley wherever space allows. It's a two-minute walk from city hall to the escarpment on the edge of town. If you like, you can climb the cut banks, pant your way straight up above the streets, sinking in fine sand, your nose full of wild sage. Sometimes I return to the campground this way, running along the top of the ridge, a windy tabletop where they built the airport.

In 1990, Whitehorse is a modern city of 22,000 with government buildings, a dozen two-storey hotels, a handsome library, ethnic restaurants, a big health food store and at least three adventure outfitters. Everything you find here is imported except a little timber and metal. Big transport trucks roll in on the Alaska Highway from Edmonton and southern cities days away; Canadian Airlines flies in and out twice a day. Originally a portage on the Klondike Trail, the city is still a frail graft on the land. In 1898, stampeders could float from the Yukon River headwaters in Lake Bennett a thousand miles to the goldfields at Dawson, except for the Whitehorse rapids, the champing waves the city is named after. The White Pass Railway solved the problem of the costly portage at Whitehorse and greatly eased the journey from Skagway. In 1959, to power the city that had sprung up from the gold rush, they built a dam that lowered the knots through Miles Canyon and brought the rearing water at Whitehorse to heel. The river is no more than a swing of fast current now, icy green, just beyond the downtown sidewalk.

Many residents are southerners with government jobs, on furlough in the Yukon. They will become smitten and stay or, after a couple of years, leave. Many are young people, young families who'll stay any way they can for the sake of raising their kids in a young place. More and more residents are Europeans, people who bring their own money and don't have to rely on the boom-or-bust economy.

THIS IS MY turn-around point, the farthest I'll get this trip. It doesn't feel like the top of a journey, the natural finish to a slow climb north. It feels more like the bottom door. From here the real north fans out—dry plains and mountains, huge, high ground I long to get at. I sniff it like a horse.

All day I trudge in the hills around the town. At night I lie in my bag with the flashlight on my chest reading *Arctic Dreams*, which I carried the whole kayak trip and up the Inside Passage, saving till now. To read it here is wonderful. I dream about polar bears wandering solitary on the ice, white on white, in a land without markers, without horizon, moving on padded feet, their snaky heads low under the big shoulder humps. Do they smell the seal under the ice? Are they following a swimming animal beneath them, waiting for a break in the ice? The female hunts with her cubs, and I picture her lying by a breathing hole, waiting all day for a seal to surface as her cubs roll and thump around her. While she waits, she's on the lookout for males. Male polar bears can be three times her size, and predatory.

I saw a photograph once, a female squatting against a block of ice, her head rolled back, nursing her cub in her arms. Polar bear skeletons resemble ours.

Lopez writes in the smallest detail about big mammals and weather and insulation. I devour his words because these details of keeping warm and dry are all I think about.

I hiked on Grey Mountain yesterday and felt my body working, the urban brain atrophied and the body woken up, large and demanding. I felt the blood come into the muscles in my legs, heat up my bones and skin, and carry me willingly all afternoon.

I spent an hour last night with Bill, the fellow who runs the campground, talking and talking for the relief of it. Then another hour in the shower building with Caroline, a woman from Toronto living in the campground for the summer. I'm idiotic with delight to have made a couple of acquaintances.

TODAY I WENT downtown and rented a car for a couple of days to drive to Atlin, the town the man in Juneau told me to see. I came off the Alaska Highway, sliding a hundred kilometres in the dust down a dead-end gravel road to this old gold-mining town on a lake, all closed up though it's only six p.m. A three-topped mountain looms like a Buddha across the water, some humpy fir islands in between. A few ribbons of pavement lined with peeling frame buildings and dipping hydro lines roll down to the shore. Ditches are stuffed with foxtail, yarrow and wild rhubarb, tall as elk. Rusty chinks of machinery, tokens from the gold rush, sink in backyards.

A couple of miles out of town I find a campground by Pine Creek, the creek that started the town, now running milky and fast through a steep gravel bed, the gold mostly emptied out. I set up close to a friendly family in the first site I see, a spot set on the bank above the poplars, the mountain filling up the view like a drive-in movie.

AUGUST 4

There's a wind-stricken kind of poplar growing here in low groves. The tight bark is waxy and engorged, the trunks nearly branchless, and the crowns like thin arms thrown over their heads, aghast. Lodgepole pine is here as well, flourishing glossy cones like scarlet fingernails. Someone has put up hand-painted signs indicating WATER, with an arrow leading down to where the creek speeds by, in case we haven't noticed.

The postmistress, who is the volunteer housekeeper of the campground, comes around to clear cigarette butts out of the firepits and replace toilet paper in the outhouses. She asks whether I've seen any little bears, as though that would be delightful, and apologizes for not being able to invite me on a boat trip that afternoon as there aren't enough seats. She explains that payment for camping goes by the honour system. I can leave my three dollars with any Atlin business.

IT'S STILL DRIZZLING when a woman wearing a garbage bag walks purposefully by in the road. I call her into my campsite for tea. She's Antoinette, a middle-aged, square-shaped sociologist from New Zealand visiting North America to investigate what makes communities healthy. She slept on Monarch Mountain last night in her garbage bag, hoping to see the sunrise. She's been here a few days, sampling all she can. "It's a pretty good place," she beams.

I leave the car in town and walk slowly around. Atlin Mountain, across the water, presides. My eyes turn to it again and again, as if taking a bearing. I feel my breathing slow. What must it be like to live in the gaze of something so beautiful?

Atlin is the most northerly town in British Columbia, set on its biggest natural lake, eighty miles long, a slender dragon of icy glacial melt. The mountains to the west roll away to the coast, to the top of the panhandle, to Alaska and the famous White Pass where thousands of people dragged furniture and horses over the mountains to get to the goldfields. A south wind prevails, blowing over an icefield and keeping the lake too stirred up most days for small craft. Over a summer there'll be a few kayaks, but it's mostly float planes, roaring in and out of town on pontoons, wobbling up into the wind and tipping delicately out of sight, barely clearing the snowcaps.

I've asked about the light this far north. At spring solstice, six weeks ago, there was no true night, just a few hours of shadowy twilight. In the winter the sun makes a weak arc in the south, the town lying in royal blue shadow by three in the afternoon before plunging into an eighteen-hour night.

I TRY A ROAD at the Tlingit end of town, which leads through cottonwood trees rearing back in an amazed, wind-bent stance, past the Tlingit cemetery to the beach. It's a rough place with low, stiff pines back of the shore and high jumbles of volcanic-looking rock on the beach, big enough to climb and dashed with bright orange and gold lichen. In pocked, brittle rock I find tiny frothy flowers.

Back in town, in front of the café, there's an old clock covered in iron curlicues, stopped at twenty past four. When I go inside, there are just a few tables under a high tin ceiling. Frank Studer, in overalls, brings me a mug of coffee and a can of evaporated milk. In a while his wife, Carol, a lanky woman with long hands and a man's wristwatch, sets down a plate of thick toast and sits at my table, pulling a hand-rolled cigarette out of her blouse pocket. I stay a couple of hours. People come and go. Carol gets them fish hooks or gummi bears—she knows everyone—and the conversation rolls along, open to all comers, gaining and losing contributers.

I go into the yard with Carol to take the weather. She shows me how she works out the cloud cover, squinting and sighting with her fingers above the mountaintop. Every two fingers is a thousand feet.

I TAKE THE CAR east of town to the cemetery, on a high ridge away from the road. The deceased have a supreme view of Atlin Mountain floating over the lake, the town a scrabble of buildings in front. To the south, Pine Creek slips in and out of the gorges like a strand of silver wire.

I walk around, looking at the graves. Some are refined and wistful, a slim painted tablet snugged next to a little pine or aspen. Most of the town seems to favour a variety of thick cement pad the size of a door, laid on the ground like a flower bed, set with plastic flower arrangements or chips of gleaming white stone resembling broken teeth. In this climate the plastic flowers have lost their spunk. The wreaths have rotted down to the Styrofoam, and the flowers have bleached to pale chartreuse or pink and strayed out of line, giving the graves a cheerful air of junk art. Frost heaves have wobbled most of the pads, arching them like old mattresses, a few so pitched you could fall into them. One or two of the graves are very inventive. What I took to be a water ski jammed in the ground is an airplane propeller.

I'M TRYING to figure out why it feels so good here. Listening tonight to Elizabeth the postmistress talk to Antoinette the sociologist helped. Not all little places are "healthy," as Antoinette calls it, but a small place can sustain a good thing if it's lucky enough to get a good thing going. Elizabeth doesn't believe people here have any superiority over people in other places, but she reckons they know one another in a different way. They are visible to one another. They know each other's habits, they have the details of behaviour. If a moose that has been frequenting the slough one winter is no longer seen, they know who likely shot it. They know who's got the flu and who hasn't been in for mail. This intimacy can be claustrophobic, but the thing about it is, nobody gets too out of hand. People are cranky or generous, but nobody's really wild. There's a kind of invisible lasso around behaviour because people can see one another and in some way are accountable to one another. Elizabeth summed it up in her practical way: "When I see some children up to something they shouldn't be doing, I go up and tell them. And I tell their mothers too."

I find out all I can, as if details would bring me in.

The town's shrunk to five hundred from five thousand a century ago, when the rush was on. There's not much work and people make do. South of town the road strays into a grotto of watercress and peters out. Being at the end of a hundred-kilometre road decides many aspects of town life. There's a tendency to stay put. The essentials are covered. There are two grocery stores, the vegetables limp and dwindled by week's end, replenished Wednesday mornings when the truck lumbers in. The gas station handles minor repairs and keeps a float of change for the laundromat. There's a liquor store, a thrift shop in the church hall Friday afternoons, a library in the courthouse twice a week. There's an elementary school on the way to the campground. Teenagers have to board in Whitehorse through the week to go to high school. There's a Red Cross station, a couple of RCMP officers, a landing field for small planes, a yard full of heavy equipment and snowploughs. The mail truck makes a run to Whitehorse three mornings a week, any weather, and takes passengers. Plumbing is unusual. People draw their water from the lake and drink it the way it comes. Everybody keeps a garden, the season swift and clamorous. Some branch out from their own garden and plant for the town—pansies in window boxes outside The Trading Post, sweet peas around the nursing station. Town chores tend to be taken care of that way, by volunteer.

AUGUST 5

I'm alone in the campground this morning, foggy air wafting off the creek, a penetrating damp. No sound but the speeding water and squirrels knocking down cones. I traced that water yesterday, taking the road to Surprise Lake, where Pine Creek starts. Signs of mining showed on the way, glimpses down the turnoffs of valleys mounded with gravel where the creek was ransacked. Old machinery stands idle like big animals put out to pasture. Surprise Lake is buried in mountains about twenty kilometres back of Atlin. I got out and stood on the bridge where the creek tips out of the lake. It leaves with plenty of flow, spreading its hand and running through bright grass, then closes, narrow and fast, bending around boulders, a winding green snake. Driving back, following it, I saw where it vanishes, choked out in a mountain of gravel. These creek beds were tossed like burgled houses, watercourses literally moved to get the gold. But this one re-emerges further down, chuckling, shape-changing, carrying on to Atlin Lake.

144 I WRAP UP my dirty tent, thank the campground for shelter, and chug the three miles into town. I'm heading for Whitehorse later on to return the car. A couple of days is all I can afford. I've been thinking about Bill, back in the campground. He saw me pulling out the other morning and asked when I'd be back. I like him. A wry, lost soul.

In town, it's overcast and still. The cloud cover has rubbed off over the lake and shows the mountain's base like a monolith, lobbed off. A man and his granddaughter in the laundromat give me a cup of detergent. While my clothes are going around, I have a cup of coffee with Carol Studer. I pack up my laundry, then drive away stunned and quiet, Mount Atlin receding in my rear-view.

And tonight I find a lover, with a body smooth as stone.

AUGUST 6

I've stopped sending postcards and letters. All of me is here. All of me is withdrawn to here.

Seven

BILL

AUGUST 12

I haven't written for a week. I couldn't. Now I'm sitting in Skagway at sea level waiting for the ferry. The Yukon's gone, over the mountains behind me, two hours' drive. A hundred years' drive.

What a town, Skagway. Even the name. A tourist town with an atrocious history, the mountains shoving it into the sea.

I want to tell about Bill, make a whole story out of the bits he gave me in six days, write about him as a way to hold on to him.

IN THE SEVENTIES Bill Armstrong ran heavy equipment in the north, built roads in raw places in B.C. and the Yukon. He spoke about it the other day, the way people mention a time in their lives when they had everything going for them.

He asked me what I was doing in 1973. I thought, making clothes for my two-year-old. Cooking dinner.

He said, "That's the year I was powering up."

Seventeen years ago. He's young to have his salad days behind him. That's the appeal of him, I think. This handsome, grieving man who thinks the best is long past.

That would have been before he married a teacher in Whitehorse and bought a house in a subdivision, before he had the two babies who are just little girls now. I didn't meet them. They came to see him once at the camp, but he was out. They left him a milkshake from Dairy Queen and a note. Probably in 1973 he had the verve for everything he was about to do. When I met him he was separated from his wife and managing the campground outside Whitehorse, a thirty-six-year-old geriatric.

He's gone, of course. He was leaving today, right after I did, for a job in Carmacks, he said.

THE ROBERT SERVICE CAMPGROUND is on a narrow strip of runty pines and bitten grass between the highway and the Yukon River, a mile south of Whitehorse. It's strictly walk-in sites; you can't bring a vehicle in. It caters to backpackers, solitary Germans and Japanese who disappear into the mountains first thing in the morning and sit scribbling at their picnic tables in the long evening, or come and go over weeks, dropping in to shower between long expeditions on the rivers or in the mountains, glamorously dirty and sunburned, rapt and uncommunicative.

There's a cinder-block bathhouse with toilets and orange Formica counters on two sides and coin-operated showers. The coin slot on the women's side sticks. I took over helping out for a few days, mucking the floors.

The office is a log cabin in a stray of pine trees with a rail porch and a few steps people like to congregate on. When I went in two weeks ago, straight off the bus from Haines, there was a crowd inside hanging around a clutter of brochures on the wall. There was an ordinary enamel fridge, stocked with beer, a Coleman stove set on a low stand, a table under the window with a registry scribbler and pencil, a metal cash box, open, and some empty coffee cups. The registry table had a wooden chair behind it and, blocking it, an old, stuffed armchair. A limp green drape covered the opening to the space in back. Behind the curtain, I found out, was a mattress on the floor and some balled-up blankets where Bill slept. That was the first of August, and Bill had been there—signing people in, answering questions, chopping firewood, swabbing the shower building, collecting garbage, loading the pop machine, opening the gate at seven in the morning and closing it at midnight—since the end of May.

He is a handsome man by any taste, with good eyes and the taut build that intolerable tension will give you. He met me kindly and signed me in, and I went on my way for a couple of days.

I DON'T KNOW many details of his life. Now I want them. He grew up in a town on the Prairies. He doesn't keep in touch with his parents or talk about them. When he was drunk once, he mentioned a brother in Toronto who plays in a symphony orchestra.

My construction is there was some wound to his confidence early on, some grievous wound, and Bill cleared out to the north like a lot of people and took up driving heavy machines, where he acquired a reputation and some pride. I wish I'd asked him about the road-building life, the lore of the heavy equipment operator. I'd like to know. In the cities, I imagine the crews aren't close; everybody disperses at night and goes home. But in the Yukon, or the top of B.C., where they build in wilderness, ploughing up rock and stumps in pristine timberland, crews camp together for weeks. There must be a culture, standards of excellence—how steep a pile of earth you can coax the tractor up without stalling, how small an axis you can whirl a hundred-tonne machine on. Is it like Harley-Davidson rallies? Or more like combat, breaking jungle trail with tanks? I bet he was good.

By the time I ran into him, the family briar patch had caught up with him or his luck had run out. He's in trouble. Sober, he has a knack for knowing what a person needs. He reads it and pulls it out of himself for you. People like to be around him, admire him—I saw that—though he never shows off, never wants to be the star. He's like a prizefighter, retired; not bitter, just not finding anything else to use up his time.

Drunk, he is dangerous.

He hustled me into the pickup the other night. It already feels so lost to me, so long gone. He was dead drunk, and put the pedal on the boards to catch the last of the sunset out on the highway, sliding in the gravel and coming to a stop so hard that I bounced into the windshield. Another time, leading some late-arriving Germans to a campsite in the dark, three sheets to the wind, he began goose-stepping and croaking the German national anthem. I watched him spend all afternoon cutting up a metal shopping cart into ragged campfire grills he threw away next day. He took out an old canoe and overturned it, spraining his ankle and leaving the boat to get lost downstream.

He let himself be robbed.

There was a kid in camp, a spooked, wild kid, who hung around the office. Bill let him stay for free in return for some chores the kid mostly didn't do. Bill lent him the keys three nights ago to get into the storeroom and didn't reclaim them before we went to bed. Before light, Bill went out to drive somebody to the airport. I was sleeping in Bill's cubby with him by then, and a few minutes after he left I heard a crash and scuffling in the office. I went naked to the doorway and saw the kid coming through the window. I stood there while he dropped to the floor, mumbled that he'd forgotten something, grabbed the cash box and ran out the door. I wrapped a caftan around me and went after him. A motorcycle roared up at the end of the road, and I saw the kid on the back of the bike behind another man, moving off, the box up under his arm. The door of the pop machine stood open, the coins gone, the keys hanging in the lock.

We made a report to the RCMP. They came out to the campground and interviewed us separately. I was dressed by then and had a glimpse of how I must appear to the officer, a middle-aged tourist shacked up with a local man Acapulco-style.

Bill said one time, in the hesitant way he had in the daytime, "I think women like a man who's—umm—a little bad." I liked this bad, sinking man with everything I had.

HE WAS PRETTY DRUNK a week ago, the afternoon I got back from Atlin. An oncoming car on the Atlin road had thrown up a ferocious spew of sharp gravel, putting out both windshields, front and back, of the rental car and scaring me half to death. Bill loopily taped garbage bags over the shattered glass and squeezed my waist. That night when he locked the gate I was still in the office, and he lit the stub of a candle and took me behind the sagging drape to the mattress where he slept. I kept my underpants on and made a night of kissing him. It's hard to find a man who'll kiss you for hours. When I finally gave him up, he threw his arm across me, knocking the breath out of me like a felled tree, and went to sleep.

I was a fairy on the road to town next morning, weightless, beatific. My lips were thick and numb, my whole skin chafed, every hair rubbed backwards and alive. I thought every step I'd come since leaving my driveway, every rain forest and croaking bird and soapberry bush and strung-up pack and sighing turn in my sleeping bag, was heading straight to this, straining me and working me to this breakout, like a thing incubating in a pond.

He does not return my ardour. He is on the other side of the moon, dulling out, the duller the better. I fascinate him, though, like the gleaming nurse who comes to the sickbed. He likes my health and enthusiasm. He told me I remind him of Audrey McLaughlin. He's a reckless choice, I know that, a person in the process of suicide.

I've been rehashing all my time with him on the wretched drive down here; the first night was the fabulous one, when he fit himself to my pleasure completely and kissed my mouth as long as I wanted.

WE HAD A QUARREL two nights ago. The yoga workshop I've signed up for in the Gulf Islands starts on August 19. With time running out before I had to leave, I got jealous of his drinking and threatened to go sleep in my tent if he kept it up. I wanted him reachable when we lay down together, but I didn't put it that way. When I warned him, he gave me a squinty look and proceeded to drink himself unconscious.

"Easy come, easy go," I said, and walked away.

For good measure I went off with another camper, a sweet boy who isn't interested in me at all but needed a drinking pal at that hour. We hiked to the power dam and listened to the roar, passing peach coolers back and forth till it got light. Then I didn't know what to do, so I hitched a ride to Haines Junction, two hours away, and hiked in the Kluane mountains until I was dying to see Bill again and begged a ride back and got there humble and eager just as he was closing the gate.

"I'm sorry. I'm so, so sorry."

He glanced at me.

"Does it mean you don't trust me?" I asked.

"Well, it changes things."

He took me back. He even made love to me, without lighting the candle, pulling me astride him with a sigh and letting me ply him sorrowfully.

But he's done. It wasn't that I mentioned his drinking. It was setting terms.

Or maybe we just had to jump hard in the puddle, break up the tender reflections, because it was time to go.

I sat across his lap this morning, a little panicky, my hand trying to take the print of his chest through his shirt. He couldn't match me. When I told him I'd miss him, he answered carefully, "I'll think of you."

And courteously he drove me to the shuttle in town, though it stops right at the gate, and no longer covering up, we watched each other coldly out of sight.

I DON'T KNOW where he is in Carmacks or even if he went there, and it is the way of things that are missing or lost that you can never finish with them. The amethyst earring rolls under the sofa and disappears, and every few years for as long as you live, you toss the living room looking for it.

And there's the suspense about his life, the juggernaut he's set rolling. You can't stop and retrace when you've gone that far. It isn't possible for Bill to go back to being a husband, to just turn in the driveway and be a dad again. He is taunting an avalanche. Some crisis is necessary, some catalyst to end or turn aside his fall, like coming into a lot of money or rolling his truck and putting out an eye or losing a father.

And not knowing how that pitch he's reached will resolve, how can I let go?

AUGUST 13

Ah Bill, farther and farther gone. Out of my need I picked you. I barely had you, barely had begun, and you're already gone. I close my eyes to keep the sight of you. Your wide-across, narrow-through body, flat and presenting like a shield, the chest the receiving plane.

Turmoil there, compressed and hot, with a deep hollow at the sternum, so much agitation. Stone limbs, the muscles under the skin engorged and taut. Your cock a slender, mobile snake.

A low walk, long arms loose and shoulders hitching forward, something hopeless or exhausted there, some collapse, some grief I wanted urgently to soothe.

Your head a little small, pulled down into your body by the neck. Deaf in one ear from a blow. Straight hair clinging to your skull, a haze of grey over the brown. Your face all eyes, not large but absorbent, the weariness spread out around them. I liked your face, your glowing, steady eyes. A Scot's face, pointed, tight reddish beard, wide clamped mouth, ground-down square teeth.

Not the oldest son, not speaking from authority, your voice low, holding your words in your chest, not elaborating. Speaking without inflection, for yourself alone, if necessary, or to draw the other away. It made me ill at ease how much you preferred me to speak. A strong man living in a wall, your whole aspect still and ready, receptive to balm or injury.

You drew me, your stillness, the constant cigarette, your body jumping with addiction, the curl of your hard hand, your habit of brief speech, your calamity. You opened when I swarmed over you and closed when I withdrew, and no second chance. Remembering bends me like an ache.

My grief is also this, the loss of me, strummed and used and blotted up in love.

Now I'm expelled and listless and have no eyes for anything. How do I recover my own skin? I don't know where it is. Nor do I want it.

I miss the sight of you, the skin of your breast, your raking breath. Too short a time.

Eight

GALIANO

Lonely. Setting up my stove tonight put a stone in my chest. Such a short reprieve. I feel like a TB patient who got to go to Arizona for a week; now I'm back with my sick lungs. I'm in Lakelse Provincial Park, east of Prince Rupert in a converted rain forest. It's a big campground, a suburb cut out of the trees, each avenue with its tidy gravel sites, each site with its firepit and shel-lacked picnic table and circle of screening trees. Only two days ago I was walking in Kluane and still had hours to go before falling through the floor.

When I left Whitehorse and took the shuttle south, time started speeding up and compressing like star travel. Leaving was like being KO'd, stunned by a blow. Nothing to do but drop.

I rode down the Inside Passage on the ferry—express this time—in a numb cocoon with a companion whose name I never asked, some telepathic woman who slept beside me all the way to Rupert and kept me company at the rail when the loudspeaker summoned us to look at orcas. I fell into Rupert again, into reunion with my car, whose door I'd unwittingly left unlocked for a month without losing anything, and into a dismaying explosion of possessions, then letters from Leon at the post office and a phone call to him where we barely remembered each other.

I couldn't find anything in town to hold me and drove out in a panic, following the Skeena River east, back to coastal trees and to this campground that I remembered from the trip out, hoping to compose myself among the thwacking axes and family barbecues. In these huge wet trees I'm like an animal wandering in a whiteout. I miss the frail spruce and vibrant Yukon peace.

I miss Bill and I miss myself—the woman springing over the ground with the high-stepping exaltation of living light and lavishing herself on a lover. I'm off that extravagance cold turkey, and it takes my breath away.

AUGUST 15

Leon fished me out of limbo today. I rode my bike through the fog to a phone booth by the lake and his voice came for me, plodding through the snow like a St. Bernard, bailing me out of the slide and setting me back in my skin again. Inserting me in a life.

He's rented the schoolhouse. This was always the plan. Without him and without the anchor of my job, there's no reason for me to stay there. I don't want to weed the driveway in his absence, or keep the garden going. I've thought about where to go. It'll have to be north. I can't live in Toronto again. I'll go to our bushlot. I'll be all right there.

We have two weeks to pack when I get home, then I'm moving and he takes off on his own adventure. There are Ontario details that claim me. The diver in free fall finally sees the X rising up to meet her.

It's raining and nothing like the Yukon. I like my campsite in the big cedars. I make my oatmeal and write to Bree. She'll be out to meet me in a few weeks. The park attendant tells me about an unadvertised hot spring in some alders nearby, and I ride my bike down to find it and loll in the steamy trench for an hour like a convalescent, the silt slowly settling on my skin.

I'll be all right now.

AUGUST 16

The unsung and reclusive Canadian Inside Passage between Prince Rupert and the northern hood of Vancouver Island is just as eye-catching as the Alaska panhandle. I drove my car onto one of the B.C. Ferries early this morning for the sixteen-hour run to Port Hardy. The ferry growls down a narrow, silky strait, the wake sending elegant swells to both shores. Low timber hills on either side bump gradually toward each other, leaving a shallow trough of sea for our passage. Clouds wind over the water like scarves and drift off the hillsides as if the trees breathed them. I sit out back in a reverie all day, taking in the landscape like food.

There's a pleased and tranquil mood on the deck after supper. The sun's making a last appearance below thick clouds, lighting the water silver and steel blue and turning the bumpy hills navy blue. They're spread wider now and we plough along, making a highway of foam. Well-dressed people walk about chatting, and look-alike couples smooch and enjoy themselves. When it gets dark, I go indoors and read the same page of my book twelve times, trying to picture Bill.

AUGUST 17

Port Hardy, on Vancouver Island. I wake up in a dripping campground newly hewed out of the bush to a view of raw stumps and fresh gravel, invisible when I came off the ferry late last night. I eat my cereal in a dry creek bed. Despite the downpour last night, there are signs it's been a dry summer. I don't really care. I'm still in a plummet that leaves me witless.

Today I'll get to Victoria and from there catch the ferry to Galiano Island, the bottom of my run. It's been a fast, hard drop.

I take the eastern shore, the lee side of Vancouver Island, heading south. My destination is a two-week yoga workshop I signed up for from home last spring. I'm not thinking about it. Yoga's an old ally. It's as good a place as any for me now.

Till noon the drive is fair, leading through a valley of fine timber, shimmering with colour after the rain. I pass many stages of regrowth, advertised by MacMillan Bloedel signs along the roadside: *Forest Forever. Replanted in 1974.* What a snow job. Everyone knows we do not harvest trees the way they do in Europe, taking only patches every hectare. In Canada we clear-cut sections so huge the land cannot hold the bared soil. Rain and wind strip it from the slopes and leave the ground too thin to support anything, till the cycle of fireweed and alder has done its humus-building. The fir sprouts that MacMillan Bloedel drops in the barren gravel will not thrive. Or if they live, their trunks will never reach the girth of trees they've harvested.

Ranting to myself and huffing carbon monoxide out my tailpipe, I drive past acre upon acre of fireweed, a soothing veil over the stumps.

South of Campbell River the shore goes into ruin. Suburbia all the way to Victoria, a fast, single-lane highway with irritating stoplights and instructions on how to interpret signals. I have noticed this about B.C. highways, the officious guidelines, as if we all don't take the car out much. To the east, the burdened water beyond the shopping malls roils brown and sulky.

It's deep twilight at eight-thirty on Swartz Bay, while I wait for the ferry. My body feels thick. I must be growing armour. It isn't safe any more to walk around with my senses basking on my skin.

AUGUST 18

Galiano. I wake up in the campground parking lot pitched next to a parked truck—all I could find in the middle of the night. I groped around for half an hour, but every campsite showed the loom of a tent or the yellow eye of a late campfire. I now see there's an available meadow fifteen feet away, but in the pitch dark I couldn't tell.

The park is a small harbour, deeply curved, like lobster pincers greeting each other. There's a trail that follows an eroding bench of ground above the shore. Several arbutus trees lean dramatically toward the slack tide; some huge spruce have already toppled. Stretches of the beach are recognizably middens, patios of tiny smashed shells built up from two thousand years of Aboriginal picnics.

The place is parched.

I circle the shore in drizzle, spotting a heron fishing and some diver waterfowl. Not loons—too high in the water for loons. Many varieties of fine bleached grasses along the trail, shivering stiffly in the low-tide breeze. I'm in love with the arbutus in spite of my resolve to stay glum for the rest of my life. It's an undulating, slinky-limbed tree with its own seasons. Now is its fall, and it is elegantly occupied shedding tough gold leaves and splitting its skin. Thin tatters of orange bark peel off to reveal a pale nudity, slippery and human-looking.

AUGUST 20

Second day of the workshop. We're on an afternoon outing to Bodega Ridge, which forms the spine of this nineteen-mile island. Getting off the property is a nice break from the density of yoga, even after two days.

Galiano is one of several Gulf Islands, all in the throes of lumbering and development. The location, just off Vancouver, is perfect for commuters, the wildness of tides and sea air an hour's ferry ride from the office. People on Galiano are well-informed and conservation-minded and know how to mount a fight. Bruce Carruthers, our teacher and host, says they've just won a battle to save this ridge from logging.

It's a gorgeous rise, covered in swishy brome, old hemlock and pine. Bruce points out Garry oak, gnarled and spreading, and manzanita ("little apple"), a witchy, tangled shrub with a purple heart and crackled outer growth, like a brittle, old-fashioned birdcage.

From the height of the ridge, to the east, we see the far-off smudge of Vancouver, and to the west, past the blue tops of firs and coasting eagles and vultures, is the hazy line of Vancouver Island.

It's a secluded place, a timbered, narrow island with the houses set secret and invisible along a narrow road that bisects the island from the ferry dock at the southern tip to the north end, where Bruce and Maureen built their house. This time of year it's all parched air, big conifers and arbutus, high drifting birds, raccoons and spiderwebs. It's the ridge, though, like a spike-backed reptile, that makes the island wild.

MAUREEN CARRUTHERS is a round, powdery woman, barely five feet tall, still British, with a beautiful bald head fizzed with white down. Her hair fell out in an attack of shingles when she was eighteen. She's a senior teacher of Iyengar yoga, a brand of hatha yoga named for an irascible Brahman teacher, B.K.S. Iyengar, still alive in Pune, India. Maureen and her husband were Iyengar's students many years ago, before Iyengar was famous. He would come and stay with them in Canada. They feel free to interpret his style of yoga in their own way. They have a mellow, experimental style of teaching that retains the exacting Iyengar form but lets breath, lightness, into the poses. Their attitude makes for a relaxed class.

We work in a splendid two-storey room with a wood floor smooth as an ice rink and glass doors that slide onto an open porch full of west weather and ocean views. The trees have been trimmed to leave a few contemplative silhouettes, then the prospect plunges to the sea, wrinkled and glinting in the distance. On the horizon is the rolling line of Vancouver Island.

The house must be the masterwork of their marriage, love's project, since there were to be no children. The design is Japanese, every detail anticipated from the bottom of the driveway to the rooftop. It stands on a rock hill, the garden lying in planes below it. You enter the yard through skinned cedar portals, climbing an arc of flagstone steps to the front door. The line of the house is long and low, at ease with the ridge. Clay tiles on the roof shed rainwater into barrels, ingenious pipes sprouting from the barrels to feed water into the garden.

The interior is simple, the whole of the house visible from either end, the walls effaced, the effect of light and quiet coming from the glowing floors and from space left empty. Outside, the west wall is all porches and views. Raked gravel inside a low wall makes a monastic perimeter before the drop over the treetops. The east side is the yard and garden—Maureen's real yoga. Continents of flowers, weltering and profuse inside their borders, are set around stone benches and stunted trees. Below them, where the ground is flat, are framed beds of splashy vegetables in black, imported soil.

On the same level as the house there's a guest cottage with a tiny kitchen and bathroom, joined to the house by a stone path. In the woods below, three circles have been cleared for tents. I choose a site full of pure yellow leaves under an arbutus. There's a blue tent already pitched, waiting for me, with a foam mat laid out inside.

AUGUST 21

Maureen met Bruce twenty years ago, when their children were grown up. She came to yoga through dance and he through a desire to understand how mind and body merge. He is a doctor in Vancouver, statuesque and silvery, with crinkly, mica-coloured eyes that don't quite focus on you. He might have fallen in love with Maureen for her yoga. She is a natural teacher, who doesn't intellectualize, who understands yoga perfectly in her body and can bring other bodies to understand it. She runs the classes, calling on Bruce in a fond and flirtatious way to provide anatomical insight to the lesson.

Having a prescribed routine to the day imposes mental quiet; that's the theory. We sign up for house chores—dusting, meal preparation, gardening. Someone walks about with a bell to signal the shift from one activity to the next. Our routine over the two weeks is this:

165

6:30   RISE

7:30   MEDITATION

8:00   SILENT BREAKFAST

9:00   MINDFUL WORK (CHORE)

10:00   WALK

11:00	ASANA (ACTIVE PRACTICE)
1:00	DINNER
2:00	OUTINGS, FREE TIME
5:00	QUIET PRACTICE
6:30	SUPPER
7:30	GROUP TIME

Today, the third day, I choose gardening. Weeding is human nature and I've been picking in the thyme beds, but Maureen sends me to clear off arbutus leaves that have scattered on the paths and shrubs. Something humble and symbolic about this chore appeals to me, the waning female cleaning up after the young, fertile one. I get absurdly involved in the zen of my chore. How many leaves to remove? How many to leave? Stem up or down?

Next in the day comes an hour's walk, the idea being to raise energy after three and a half hours of communal silence. The runners in the group go out on the paved road below the house and sprint off. I sit beside my tent in my circle of fallen leaves, doing nothing.

My favourite is asana practice. If my body could stand it, I'd do yoga all day. It's the great escape, the great quieter of fuss and bother.

I WENT TO MY FIRST CLASS eight years ago on the say-so of a friend, having no experience and no preconceptions. There is a yoga centre in Toronto, up a steep flight of stairs on Yonge Street, in operation since the early seventies and presided over by a sixty-year-old mother of six, Marlene Mawhinney. We spent half an hour that first class jackknifed over our knees, clenching our quadriceps, while Marlene, in a loud voice from the front of the room, exhorted us to "lift the knees." I had no idea how to do that without using my hands, but the internal concentration, the activity of intently and undividedly instructing muscle, willing muscle to obey, was the most refreshing thing I'd ever done.

Yoga is precise. It is directed action, verb and object. There isn't anything else going on except the mind, deep in its cave, telling the body what to do. The command in a pose to "reach into the fingertips" is everything you are doing at that moment. The effect is euphoric.

It sounds psychological more than physical, and perhaps it is. Or it's both. Mr. Iyengar says, "Don't run, don't get massage, don't see a psychiatrist, *don't* do aerobics—practise yoga."

On the physical plane, yoga stretches the muscles and tendons so that you have more range of motion. You can look further over your shoulder, you can get your arms straight above your head, you can bend from the hips to tie your shoe. It's the antidote to aging. It counteracts the body's natural bowing and tightening. The more you stretch muscle and tendons, the more the bones ease into alignment. When a bone moves into its proper place after years of being infinitesimally askew, there's a release that can make you cry. I've burst into sobs in warrior pose more than once, my sacrum shouting hallelujah.

Inversions, the upside-down poses, give the organs a rest and allow gravity to coax them the other way. Twists tone the kidneys. Back bends stretch the intestines and gut as well as reverse the bend of the spine and let it breathe. The postures ply and stimulate the organs and work on the nervous system in ways I don't understand, but there are effects and emotions associated with the poses that are predictable, that you can bring to bear to alter your state of mind. Headstands and back bends raise energy. Blood into the chest, as in shoulder stands and the doubled-over poses, calms and steadies.

Slowly, slowly, the muscles tone, the skin starts to come alive and glow.

Because practice is rigorous, enjoining you to push muscle and bone to the farthest edge the tendons will allow, because you're taken up, the brain is quiet. You can't fidget or plan a meal in a back bend.

Maureen is good at imparting the idea that yoga is personal; there's no standard. There is the assumption that regular practice is desirable, but how one performs the postures is a long continuum.

There is "correct action" in every pose, a direction it must tend, but where each body locates itself along that direction is different and doesn't matter. In class Maureen demonstrates the pose and says all she can about the experience of it. The choice of words is important. Poses are always done from the inside out. Your focus is inside your body—there in the hip socket, in the sinew at the back of the knees—not out in the room, looking on. Images can help you enter the joints where the movement is: "Spin the leg bones outward." "Press the palms on the floor like suction cups."

When she's said all she can, we work the posture on our own. Maureen and Bruce and Anna, their assistant, come around to make adjustments. They study our effort in the pose, correct with their hands or words, always following the trajectory, the direction of movement, so there's no jarring.

TODAY WE WORK the standing poses and I have my usual discouragement at not being able to reach my extended back heel to the ground. I've tended to walk on tiptoe all my life, and by now my Achilles tendon is past remedy.

In the mornings Bruce leads us in pranayama, breathing practice. I find it excruciating. It is nearly impossible to sit perfectly still for half an hour supporting your own weight, keeping your mind "quiet" while your legs go numb. In the sixties, when everybody meditated,

I remember seeing people at weekend workshops folded pallid and waxy on gymnasium floors, their chests hardly stirring, vanished to some other zone. I try to guess, of my present companions, who has a quiet mind and who, like me, wanders and returns, wanders and returns, listens to the birds, grasps at straws, daydreams.

It's something we don't discuss. We're just supposed to get the hang of it. Like having orgasms. There is a ban on revealing pranayama failure. We have a self-imposed seriousness about sitting every morning, I don't know why. Possibly we're saving face, showing that we're good retreatists and can put up with going numb.

I never miss sitting practice in the morning. I come for the wrong reasons. I love the gloom in the room and the aesthetics of the rough blankets we drape around ourselves and the increasingly idiosyncratic arrangements of pads and bolsters we devise to prop our spines. I like the ping of the brass bowl Bruce taps with the little padded wand and the collective sigh as we begin. I like meandering along the moments, falling into landscapes and pursuing a visual thread over open ground, giving way little by little to panoramic views, to full-out northern tripping, gliding over tundra and icefields, then recovering myself, like falling through a crack, and minutely straightening my back and beginning once again. Morning pranayama comes to be a time for gorgeous outings, illegal and unimpeded.

AUGUST 22

The orderliness of our life thrills me. There is the illusion of purpose in these measured activities. I find myself planning a routine to live by when I get home:

10:00—11:00   GARDEN THE WOODLOT

2:00—3:00   GOOD DEEDS (E.G. LAND CLAIMS)

A drawback of the tinkling bells and healthy food is a raging appetite for sex. I'm on spikes no matter what I do. I crave a lover. I wish Bill had been less enervated when I knew him. Really, he was about done in by the time I showed up.

AUGUST 23

I'm writing from a pile of slithery arbutus leaves, propped against a fallen log in shifting light. A cool, still morning gave way to sun this afternoon, and everyone's gone horseback riding. Maureen is trying out her new hose, watering the arbutus and impatiens from the rain barrel. Bruce is at some task, crinkling his eyes at me as I pass, absent but friendly. My grove blooms with cobwebs.

I set the thousand images of the north before my eyes whenever I'm alone, absorbing and leaving them over and over, like endlessly kissing someone goodbye. If I went back . . . there's no going back. The days are shorter now. Caroline, my pal from Whitehorse, is no longer living in her tent, Bill has gone to Carmacks or somewhere. What I'm so attached to isn't there. I feel wistful looking at the cobwebs. Not resisting any more, not distressed, but sad.

And menopausal to boot. Intense sweats several times a day. I don't like the heat, metallic and bitter. And there's some emotion too, some tumult. If estrogen is on the ebb, how much does estrogen have to do with me? What if it's a substance I really need? What if it's part of confidence or generosity, or an ingredient in humour? What part of me is dying?

I have a hunch it's sex, that dear snake in the grass I'd hate to lose. There's a sinewy, yearning kind of sexuality that's mine, and when I think of it gone, I can't imagine who I'll be.

AUGUST 26

I've been reading a book of Bruce's about Ayurvedic medicine. Prakriti is an ancient Eastern system of prescription suiting certain diets and lifestyles to constitutional types. I love its physicality. Constitutional types are defined by the quality of skin, hair and nails, how much you sweat, what your shit is like.

Instructions are very specific. For Veda types: "Limit raw foods. Astringent fruits should be baked or stewed. If you must eat legumes, first soak them and throw away the soaking water. Cook with turmeric, cumin and coriander. Garlic and ginger are especially good.

Always use a little oil, for insulation. Of nuts and seeds, almonds are best, sesame products ruin tone in the digestive tract."

Such confidence. Thousands of years of human observation. All we Europeans brought to the New World was cannons.

I read, "Anything can be a meditation, as long as it is sincere and heartfelt. Meditate on the rising sun. Wash the body before meditation—at least the sense organs and the feet."

I revise my planned routine:

RISE AND WASH

SIT FOR FIFTEEN MINUTES

BREATHE FOR FIFTEEN MINUTES

HAVE TEA AND BREAKFAST

DO MINDFUL WORK

DO YOGA

SLEEP WITH HEAD TO THE EAST

It's normal for yoga retreats to produce introspection. I've tried valiantly to recall one detail about who attended this particular retreat, but except for a couple I already knew who run a restaurant in Toronto, I remember nothing about anyone. I was out of it, hoarding myself. There was something I was trying to hold on to that I thought socializing would drive off. I was afraid the whole love affair with the Yukon would dissipate and float away—the images, the sense of myself as intact—if I let myself loll in a deck chair and chat with somebody.

AUGUST 27

The workshop is ending. I'm not sorry to go. I woke up with a sore throat, catching sick being around people. I'm worried how I'll do with Bree. She's a lot of company all at once. Maybe I'll be ready. This morning, for the first time in pranayama, my mind did not speed to the Yukon. I could bear seconds at a time in empty space.

The clutter of Birkenstocks at the front door gradually dwindles for the last time. We haul our duffles to the van. Maureen has covered her head in a gesture of parting, and I've patted the arbutus leaves in my tent circle goodbye.

I have two days with friends in Victoria and then Bree.

Nine

GOING HOME

We have our first fight on the ferry to Victoria. It's about who was supposed to bring rain gear for her.

"You *said* just bring yourself."

"It's a figure of speech, Bree."

She hates my irritation and is uncanny at detecting it. We do this after every separation. It's like a blister on the live skin between us that starts swelling the minute we're together. Or maybe it's just the rough, big-mammal way I lick her off and claim her.

I was thrilled to see her at the airport, arriving on a night flight from Toronto, tanned and glamorously dishevelled, fragrant of stale air and Body Shop and Trident gum. A young man in a rower's jersey who sat next to her on the flight moves off wistfully. She grins and shrugs.

I've met Bree off a hundred public conveyances—off trains all through high school, when she went to boarding school in the

Eastern Townships, off camp buses every summer, off planes now that she's older. It used to be she'd billow through the Arrivals door already talking or crying—effusing, one way or another, even in her teens. I liked that. It bridged any awkwardness or strain her absence might have accumulated. Now she's nineteen and has sprouted antennae I would never have predicted. She advances smiling and composed. "Mom, you look so well."

Gathering her things and heading out the sliding doors, I don't know what to do with all the space she's left me.

Jeremy and Dalla have lent us their van for the trip to the airport so we'll have a place to sleep. Bree's plane arrived too late for us to catch the last ferry back to Victoria. I park on the causeway at Tsawwassen as far from the fluorescent lamps as possible and we crawl in back under some limp quilts their old dog sleeps on. When I hear Bree sigh with contentment, I recognize her. This girl doesn't mind where we bed down. She's never minded.

As a baby she'd stand in her crib in the morning in an icy diaper, crowing with delight. When she was four and I'd take her camping, she'd come undone somehow in the night, ease out of her sleeping bag and off the sleep mat. By morning she'd be sprawled, coverless, under the sagging tent wall on the bare floor, nose tilted, breathing frosty puffs.

I snug beside her in the van, hoping we'll be fine.

AUGUST 30

I'm on one of the famed beaches in Pacific Rim National Park, the sun back at the road, not yet arrived. There's no one here. Bree's up the road in Tofino, asleep in the motel.

The drive was fine. It was consoling to return the fumy van to Jeremy and reclaim my old Mazda. My car has been our living room for years, the place we're most at home. Bree fed the tape deck, we bought figs and rolls and Jarlsberg cheese at the halfway point, and stopped for an hour on the highway farther on, in Cathedral Grove, an old stand of Douglas fir, straight and fragile as the Parthenon.

When we reached the coast the weather turned rainy, and we gave up camping on the beach and went on to Tofino to a motel.

MOST OF THIS last precious swath of temperate rain forest is now parkland, edgily protected by conservationists. There is always the threat of encroachment, and Tofino, a fishing village at the top of the park, is regularly down a few citizens who've gone to jail for protesting. Confrontations with loggers are viewed as part of the town's upkeep. When we drove in last evening, the town's feisty spirit seemed subdued. It's the end of the season and raining, just a few restaurants and guest houses open, desultory proprietors stirring around like tired hosts after a party.

I CREPT OUT to the beach this morning over a jungle trail. Sea air and rainfall on this side of the island nurse the trees to outrageous size. Ferns and shrubs grow in an uproar. The cedars look like Amazon rubber trees drooping tropical lianas. Sitka spruce raise monstrous trunks against the spraying sea.

I've been dying to show Bree, but she's asleep. I left her this morning, dim and muzzy in the motel bed. I forget this detail about our reunions, that she spends the first two days asleep. I should plan for it, move us both into a cave for forty-eight hours to acclimatize. Instead, I have a list of things I want to show her: this Sitka, its fish-scale bark glowing purple, this enormous skunk cabbage, these banana slugs the size of . . . bananas.

The tide is out, its roar way off as I start to walk. I'm ruminating about something Barry Lopez wrote in his book about the North: the idea of being connected—not just associated, but deeply in conjunction with the physical world. He was intrigued by the Inuit he stayed with in the Arctic. It seemed to him they have a simple, concrete relationship with their world that does not analyze or interpret, that is released from what a thing "means" to what it "is." He thought the Inuit did not distinguish between animate and inanimate. For them, all things are composed of the same jumble of living matter, in one arrangement or another.

I am struck by a culture that orients more to non-difference than to difference, that perceives of a small boy, say, as a variation on a fox or an ice floe. A natural relation for human beings with land, I think. Natural and yet unusual, because our urban North American power of discernment is overdeveloped. Our brains teem with the activity of ruling out, eliminating, selecting, discriminating, a habit we practise a thousand times a day that gives us the false idea that the objects of the world are separate from each other and from us. We think a bear is not the same thing as a human or a skunk cabbage. Yet physical science, if you don't like New Age, tells us that we *are* in fact all one. A bear and a skunk cabbage are much more the same than they are different. What would it be like, I wonder, if our first thought, regarding anything, was to perceive the kinship, the non-distinction, rather than shorting out to the difference between things?

Walking along the beach, I think this might be the gem in my experience this summer, the lesson I have to sustain me when I'm home and thinking about the next thing to do with myself. I had a glimpse of something this summer. There was the exhilaration of the views, the extravagant layout for the senses each day, but I also got an inkling of the join, the non-difference. There were a few seconds somewhere—maybe in the Yukon or Atlin or on that high plain out of Haines—a few seconds when my whole being relaxed, when I was held in the land, not separate and apart but in it, just another sentient creature, another form of shrub or mountain.

If there's no difference, if I am that—a kind of mountain, a bush that moves—then I don't have to be afraid to die. I can go home. If I am endless and inconsequential, a flake of mountain that thins and blows away, where is the loss? The mountain is always coming and going.

Now the sun's arriving full, the surf scrambling in. I hurry back to Bree.

SEPTEMBER 2

The second day in Tofino I lost my voice. The bug I got on Galiano hit emotional pay dirt in my throat and I couldn't say a word.

The whole town is slumped in the rain. We've walked in the old forests on Meares Island and in the wet streets in town; we've watched the big tide lift and lower the moored boats at the dock. Bree sleeps, I rasp, we eat a lot of meals.

While we walk in the rain, getting used to each other, I'm in a turmoil of resistance. I don't want my freedom to end. Once I leave here the road is all homeward bound, and when I peer down the kaleidoscope at what's ahead, the days look fractured. I don't want to take up whatever's next. Out here on the farthest rim of the country, I feel as though I'm backpaddling above a waterfall. Even Bree looks to me like a beloved and devouring sea.

She and I are like people in love with each other who never get to live together and calm down. It's been like this since she was fifteen. She went away to boarding school after the uprising with her father and I'd see her on holidays or when Leon and I would drive seven hours to Lennoxville to visit her in her tunic and routines at school. From the age of ten she went away every summer to camp. This past year, when she was finishing high school, she lived in Toronto. Time together is always an occasion. It takes us days to settle down, get the bond tuned up and do what people who live together are practised at doing: be by ourselves in each other's presence. This time especially, after my summer as the Lone Ranger, I'm waiting for the intensity to ease, the engine to settle down to an idle.

SEPTEMBER 3

We're in Vancouver and I'm disoriented, to put it mildly. Last night I drove miles out of our way to a campground I was determined to find, which turned out to be a chain-link RV lot, picturesquely located next to an airstrip.

Dazed and wretched in Labour Day traffic today, I haven't the wits to keep Bree and myself clear of mother-daughter undertow, and we sink into our classic fight.

I'm thinking ahead to university for her next year, and I want to go over to UBC to see what we can find out. Bree wants to shop for crystals on Granville Island. I wonder (out loud, mewling slightly) how she can pass up a visit to the university, since we're here. At least pick up a catalogue.

"We don't need to go there, I know all about it."

"How could you know? We haven't been there."

"I've already decided I want to come to school here. They've got what I want."

"What?"

"Mountains."

This is not a serious person. I can't reconcile myself to her approach to things, and we have the awful and familiar fight where she accuses me of lack of trust and I lie and deny it.

Like most mothers, I'm taking my time releasing my child. It's a long business, requiring that I pretend she is ill-equipped for independence. I worry that she is not ready for the world, that she sleeps too long, is too fond of fun. I worry she lacks a sense of scarcity she's going to need in the world. This is pure rationalization, of course. In truth, I just can't let her be. I want to keep prodding the wet clay into the shape I have in mind. I commentate, make suggestions, try to modify what she does, and Bree takes this as an insult.

I know this is an ordinary renegotiation of who runs Bree's life. This is the normal-as-pie, monumental psychological work of releasing a grown child, an expectation that human beings probably can't accomplish at all. In action, the transition looks like a gloves-off battle for control. There's a twist to it, though, that makes it especially fraught. The twist is, mothers never understand their power. I learned this from my families at the counselling agency. In the battle with our daughters, we think our daughters have the edge. They seem cocksure and heedless and too bold, and we think whatever influence we can bring to bear is fair game. Because we don't feel strong in our forties. We're aging, newly aging, and in this culture that's only bad news. We're not used to it yet, we don't sense any of the gains we'll feel later on. In our forties we're grouchy and off-kilter and appalled. It would be better if the thirty-two-year-old aunt or the grandmother took over and tussled with our teenage daughters for a few years, let us sit it out.

The fifth decade is the small death for women. When we look around, it can seem as though everything we're losing has landed squarely on our adolescent daughters. They've got looks, nerve, a full head of steam, while we're sunk in duty, caring for others, keeping the balls in the air, watching our skin go slack. I'm not saying we're jealous or anything simple, but we're in a tricky patch. For a while we don't know our own strength, and in our protest and dismay our lovely, moody daughters, already trained mirrors, take the heat.

It's never a fair fight, though. We always have the edge, no matter how frayed and besieged we think we are, because they need our approbation. We have an open channel to our children's self-esteem and we always will. It's never a fair fight.

Sometimes I know this and sometimes I don't. I should have known it today. Haven't I just lost a husband and a lover and the out-of-doors? I should know to stand clear of a fight.

In this quarrel my sense of righteousness fades fast. My argument is not really with Bree. She doesn't let me off, though. I have to drag around smacking myself in the forehead till we're both tired of it.

We walk around Granville Island in a cruelly brilliant sun, not speaking, and she buys a rock from Uranus, or somewhere dense and heavy.

SEPTEMBER 4

We escape Vancouver. We're back in landscape and truly heading home, climbing north, following the Fraser River to join the Yellowhead Highway. From here, it's steady east. We spend the morning in the shadow of the Cascades, dark, faulted mountains dropping straight into the Fraser River. Then we follow the Thompson River till the pitched black rock lets into rolling mountain and broad valleys. We stop to picnic beside a long rumple of bleached grass going off into flecked hills. The dry air blows hot gusts of sage, and I think of the tawny pass at Haines and the grey-green bluffs at Whitehorse. Of all climates and geography, bare hills, too dry and lumpy to cultivate, are my favourite.

SEPTEMBER 7

For the thousandth time I watch the sun on timber slopes and let the colour soak into my eyes. We've climbed the last of the route north and must turn east. I'm deep in memory. It's been very strong again the last two days. I hate to turn away. Staring at these mountains all summer, the swag of trees over rock, I'm joined to them. I feel myself leave my body now and go to them, the way I've done a hundred times. All my cells lie in the trees, and I have their life. The air stirs the top boughs, the clouds moisten the needles, birds scream close by, light and dusk revolve. I don't give up the joining. I turn away and steer the car east, and in the centre of my head I stay there on the flank of the mountain.

OCTOBER 7

My journal has petered out. Now I'm setting mousetraps in my house; maple leaves are falling off the trees.

The drive went pretty well. It was early fall, the land cooling off and growing dark. Bree and I cooked our suppers wearing headlamps, the picnic table, the ground, the tent flaring up in yellow circles. Wheat fields I'd seen black and rolling over in farmers' furrows in June had had their season and stood bone white again, a huge shorn disk around us.

We had a spiritual experience in Elk Island Park, past Edmonton. Buffalo roamed the campground, browsing the grass, unpenned and mingling with the few end-of-season visitors. One was standing, gigantic, outside the tent when I crawled out, his lovely liquid eye reproachful.

We ate picnics, spread on the hood of the car or on the ground. When we stopped at dusk we had packaged soups—minestrone thickened with leftover oil from a can of smoked oysters—cookies from the health food store.

I did the driving; Bree chose the music. I replayed the North in the roominess of my mind. We grew tolerant of each other and wry. I had my head inside the tent one morning, waking her. She began telling me a dream, a long one, and after a few minutes, without meaning to, I tuned out. In the middle of her recounting I backed out of the tent and walked away. She said, "We should have sent God out here to meet you."

Ontario was raining. We drove the whole Superior sweep from Red Rock to Agawa Bay in blackout, after nightfall. We woke bleary on a cobble beach, seagulls strutting up and down, a turquoise counterpane jiggling in front of us, completely by ourselves. We stuck around, rock-hopping, taking pictures; then a fog blew in and we drove on.

At the end we left Highway 17 and took the ferry from Tobermory. It was cold and wild, but we stayed outdoors, sitting on a storage bin on deck, pressed together, Bree invisible in her hood except for the tip of her nose.

SHE GOT A JOB in Montreal when we got home. Leon greeted me skittishly and we took up our friendship, but there wasn't much to say. I didn't know what to tell. I don't know what to make of things myself. I'm nothing articulate. I'm huge pictures ballooning and subsiding, not much else. I wrote to Bill, but my letter came back unclaimed.

Leon and I spent two weeks packing the schoolhouse and the new people moved in. They will rent for a year. Then we'll decide.

Leon left for California a week ago and I came here, to the house on our property I haven't stayed in before, a square house set high on the hill, crowded in by trees. I brought the big gas stove, my rocking chair, Leon's frail Persian rugs and our two cats. He left me in my towers of cardboard cartons and I unpacked myself.

The leaves on the maples in the yard rub each other endlessly and bob in the gold air. I'm in my house, walking around my rooms, still turning like a dog on a rug who can't make up his mind to lie down, still held in the North.

Ten

LATER ON

I forget how pale the Yukon is. Flying from Life-Saver green Ontario in late May or June and landing in these long, sere views always feels strange, as though setting down in a country drained of colour.

We float down through thick, soaked cloud, the ground gradually coming up, dirty ice clogging the Yukon River, tracks of yellow-green spruce like a vast nubby ground-sweater jabbing up. In Whitehorse the land is barely stirring after winter. I gather my belongings and get out of the terminal building. The air is chilly. The snow has gone off and at the edge of the parking lot I see where the Yukon sets in, the pale ground wandered over by bleached grasses and wild sage, loose stone and huddles of willow, a huge, poor land in tones of pale silver and gold at any season.

I'm on my way to Atlin. This will be the eighth time since the first excursion ten years ago, when I rented a car in Whitehorse and drove down on the say-so of the man in Juneau. I came again the following spring, 1991, flying that time, and went on to Atlin for a night or two. Carol Studer's husband had died in the meantime and she took me for a drive in their old brown van, noting that it was the first time she'd started up an automobile in twenty-three years. "Frank didn't like me to drive."

On that trip I got up onto the Dempster Highway by pure luck, hitching a lift out of Dawson City and riding to the Arctic Circle in mid-June, when there is no night.

Then I came four years later, in 1995. I took three months off work and drove my car to Atlin for the summer, and since then the visits have bunched up to every nine or ten months, one season or another. This is a place where I've made a rough nest, a mud-and-twigs home that I come back to and that I hold in my mind when I'm in Ontario. I have outlasted the urge to buy property and move here, which I could not do. I come back, though, and by now I've patched together all the phases of light and growth in this part of the north, laying the seasons end to end, except for the freeze-up in November and December. I've never seen the grey sky lie down on the face of the lake and hang there till the ice forms. I've arrived when the lupines cover the ground in purple, and this time, on the way to my rental car, I see them barely in bud, holding water drops in star leaves.

When I'm at home, buried in my life, I long for Atlin. I see the wide cradle of sky between Monarch and Atlin mountains, the dipping line they make meeting each other, and I pine to be there. I arrange to go, by hook or by crook, and have a minute of elation when the leave from work is set or the flight booked. Then the plan begins to seem undoable, extravagant. So far to come just to walk about for a few weeks. But I come, and it seems settled that I always will. Lawrence Millman calls these unused territories "last places." There are others I would like to visit, but I have a root here and I keep it tended. Atlin rocks me. I come around the corner, the last bend in the beat-up road from Jakes Corner, past the Atlin Unincorporated sign, and the view of Atlin Mountain smacks me in the face, its three draped snow tops, its gravel sickle, its huge bulk thrumming the sky, and every cell of me starts to quiet down and spread out at that moment.

I have only three weeks this time, little enough that I had to fly. Today is Sunday and there will be no mail truck to take me down to Atlin till Wednesday. I've rented a car so I can get out of town into the mountains while I wait.

MAY 22, 2000

I'm sitting in my sleeping bag in the back seat of the Chevy Cavalier I've rented. I took a turn off the road to Carcross last evening and came down a new gravel road that ends at a lake skirted by white dirt hills. I found a hollow in some willows where I parked. Lacking a tent, I slept in back, cranked on the fold-down seat like a hospital patient. I'm under-slept and longing for tea, looking out my six windows. The rising sun is beginning to wash the mountains to the west, lighting the hollows and scapes of snow. Willow beside me has a new growth of shiny mahogany in the grey crackle of the old. Past it, a mat of blond grass drops off into a gully of willow, wiry and fine like a bundle of hair. There's a small grey lake beyond, just free of ice. Last night there were ducks on it and a pair of terns hopscotching and shrieking above the surface. The ground is pale, fine dirt in a caked winter shape that poofs and breaks up under my step. A pointy band of amber spruce runs to the lap of the mountains. The mountainsides veer up, umber-coloured rock heaving clear of the treeline, angling into the clouds, grabbing the slow-passing clouds, and dabbing them to their cold, extraordinary faces. Mountains do everything for their own sake.

My body is still on Ontario time. I've been awake since four-thirty, shivering and happy. I love these long Yukon views, the beautiful undisturbed land in all its verve flowing away to the edge of sight.

Pitching in or near a vehicle is frowned upon by outdoors people, but what about living in an egg, a protective steel egg that moves from place to place? What about travelling in a shell?

I reach Carcross before eight. The roadside gas station and mini-mart is open, and I wait for the boy to come down and turn on the burner for tea. The town has a spectacular setting, lying in a narrows between Bennett and Tagish lakes, a wide junction where the mountains jump out of flat ground. Like so many settlements up here, Carcross was a hunt camp until the gold rush pumped it to size.

Today the town is at low ebb, even as a historical site. Carcross lost its centrepiece several years ago when its steamboat, the *Tutshi*, burned. The ferry had its heyday during World War I when well-to-do Americans were looking for an alternative to travelling in Europe and sought holidays in the north. Visitors would come up the coast by steamer to Skagway and from tidewater take the railway over the White Pass into the Klondike. As a pleasant detour travellers transferred at Carcross to the *Tutshi* and were ferried east across Tagish Lake through Taku Arm to a little portage, where they would hop on a train to Scotia, to the dock on Atlin Lake, and then be ferried on the *Tarahne* to town. The *Tarahne* still stands in dry dock on the waterfront in Atlin, fresh white paint lashed over her rotting sides. In town, in those days, visitors were dined and put up in style at the White Pass Hotel before returning the way they came to resume their journey north. The Depression ended this three-day excursion and the careers of the *Tutshi* and *Tarahne*. The famous railway/water route between the

White Pass and Atlin has thinned now to a ghost trail, etched again every once in a while when a dogsled team races over it.

CARCROSS IS OUT OF BUSINESS and looks particularly dispirited at the moment, with Nares Lake virtually empty of water across from the mini-mart. At this time of year the lakes are at their lowest level, the nights still too cold to melt the surrounding glaciers. Once the runoff starts, the lakes will gradually fill, and by August they'll look themselves. Nares is a spongy meadow at the moment, floating a few cheerful ducks in its puddles.

The proprietor is the same blond bear-man as always, the owner of a kind-hearted orange dog everybody always asks about when they've been away. Local people begin to file in, looking a little sunken after a winter of wan light and no work.

When I first came up here I was afraid to talk to people. I thought getting into conversation would waylay me, break my association with nature, which felt frail as cobwebs at the time. I had an anxious, hoarding feeling when I travelled here ten years ago, as if I might lose at any moment something I'd got hold of that I really needed. Now it is a pleasure to talk to people. Now I am fastened to the out-of-doors by piano wire.

The proprietor is slumped in a plastic chair, talking about the economy in a tired, unemphatic voice, the eastern sun frisking over the empty lake, setting off dust motes in the mini-mart. There aren't enough investors, he says, not enough dollars going into finding new mineral deposits, the holdout gold and silver pockets, wherever they may be. It's mostly all family prospecting now, small claims. Timber isn't much this far north. It'll have to be tourism, which the Yukon is a funny spot for, from most people's point of view, being a wedge of territory on the way to Alaska. It just isn't convenient to leave the Alaska Highway and go up to Dawson City, say, five hundred kilometres north; nothing but trees till you get there. Gas being the price it is, not many people will bother.

He tells me the Yukon makes about a hundred dollars a day per mobile home rolling through to Denali Park—a hundred dollars in gasoline and bottled juice. Nothing at all off the buses.

ALASKA, ON THE OTHER HAND, is a glutton for tourism. I see evidence at the bottom of the White Pass when I drive over the U.S. border down to Skagway, mile zero of the Goldrush Trail. My destination is Haines, a forty-five-minute boat ride down the Lynn Canal, but the shuttle to Haines doesn't leave until five. In Skagway the mountains pitch straight into the ocean, there is no beach to speak of, nowhere to go but the half-mile stroll through town, which is a pure tourist arcade. At the height of the season there might be four cruise ships a day in the ports between Prince Rupert and Skagway. The *Princess* is in today, a ship the size of four apartment buildings, a floating wall, no resemblance to a sea-going vessel. I can't think what it would do in weather.

It looks like these panhandle towns are being trained into ruin by tourism. Twenty or so of them lie between here and Ketchikan— a handful of little coastal communities isolated from one another except by sea, occupied for thousands of years by Aboriginals who lightly pillaged the water and forests, then by whites, who pillaged hard and, along the way, worked themselves into tight-knit little villages with their own character and particular hardiness. Now they're up to nothing but fobbing off souvenir baseball caps and "fossil" pendants on wave after wave of tourists streaming off cruise ships in Nike running shoes.

Haines is keeping a better grip on itself. There is still some diversity in Haines, with its creaky eagles, sprawled under gigantic mountains. I get here in the evening, the catamaran shuttle *Fairweather* slamming over big swells in Lynn Canal against a ferocious south wind. In my kayak I wouldn't stand a chance. Human horsepower is about half a knot.

I walk up to the Halsingland, part of the old Fort Seward, a wooden hotel that keeps a few low-end rooms without baths, splendid enough for me, with fifteen-foot ceilings and tall, rattly windows that look out on the bay. I've stayed here a couple of times, most recently last year when I came in April, before the hotel was really open. I arrived off the ferry late at night. I had called ahead, but when I arrived there was no one at reception and the desk was shuttered closed. No one around at all, not a sound, but I found an envelope propped in the corner addressed *Jill*, with a key in it and a note: *If you need anything, call Louise. Good night.*

MAY 23

I recross into the Yukon tonight after a perfect day rock-grubbing in the intertidal zone at Haines. I come over the White Pass in the gold of evening, my eyes everywhere and the window rolled down, though it's freezing. The ziggly poplars that never grow straight are in glistening bud, still tight and sticky, barely there.

Tagish and Tutshi lakes have broken free of ice, a change that happened overnight. When I came down yesterday the lakes were all black shadows under a grey skin of ice, torn open at the shore. Further on, where they fronted the wind, the lakes were blown open straight across, a frothed, thin edge of ice driving down the water, harried by the north-rushing wind, the crinkled, black water shining and flying at a thin veil of ice, like old silk over the loosening water. It was a live thing, the breakup. This evening it is accomplished: there is no more ice. The water jiggles innocently north in its summer shape, no memory of confinement.

I pass a grizzly bear, snorfing by the roadside.

ATLIN IS A gold rush town. Partners, two young men in their

twenties, one from Nova Scotia and one from Juneau, found the black sand that heralds gold in a creek bed running into Atlin Lake late in the winter of 1898. The gold rush to the Klondike was in full swing a few mountains away. When news broke about the Atlin find, thousands of people struggling over the Chilkoot Trail, along with most of the work crew engaged in building the White Pass Railway, walked away from their endeavours overnight and headed east to Pine Creek. In the last months of the season the town of Atlin burst into being.

It lies at the mouth of Pine Creek halfway up Atlin Lake, an enormous glacial string bean, its southern tip straying into the gravel fingers and islands at the foot of Llewellyn Glacier and its northern end reaching into the Yukon. Other than the reserve at Five Mile, south of town, there is no other settlement on the lake. Inland Tlingit probably had known the district for centuries, had trapped there or made summer camps, but only a handful of white prospectors likely ever reached the lake prior to the gold rush. It lies in the Coast Mountains, two thousand feet above sea level, entirely different in character from the coast two hundred miles away. Atlin is dry, climatically semi-arid, with thin, stony ground and low, wind-stricken trees, mainly spruce and pine, alder and cottonwood. Any abrasion to its surface takes a long time to heal.

At its peak there were five thousand Atlin residents. The boom was short-lived, but the town prospered and managed to hang on as a tourist attraction till the Great Depression put the White Pass and Yukon Railway Hotel out of business and the town's ferry in dry dock. By the forties and fifties there were only about a hundred residents, clinging on without economic prospects of any kind. In the sixties, with gold at something like ninety dollars an ounce and a cultural movement underway that had people roaming around looking for uplifting places, Atlin began a revival. Small prospecting perked up and a handful of artists moved in, setting up in the squatters' cabins along the shore or, if they had money, picking sites for themselves in the surrounding hills and building log houses. Today there are about five hundred Atlin souls.

MAY 24

Four o'clock. It's my birthday and I'm in my yard—here again— Atlin Mountain shimmering in late, high sun, a raven extemporizing on the flagpole at the weather station next door. He makes a roughed-up silhouette doing his spring repertoire: tut-tuts, wet chortles, barking dog impersonations. My yard has a tilt, a gentle grade from the hedge to the shed and little buildings where I stay. At the moment the yard is shivering with young dandelion leaves, wild rose stubble and filaments of last year's grass. The hedge is barely in bud, and for once I can see through it to the road.

Joyce has left me keys to both buildings and I've taken the cabin, the smaller place, a square, uninsulated room lined with wood like a cigar box, the door facing west. In the mornings this room is freezing, but by afternoon I can open the door and the sun will gradually crawl in and fill the room. By suppertime, when I'm standing at the counter making dinner, the heat hits hot on the backs of my knees.

My room has white curtains on rings that I draw across the windows at night as a cue that it's time to sleep. There will be no true dark this time of year. The fridge is in the corner with an Arborite table beside it and three matching vinyl-and-metal chairs, the stuffing coming through the seats in a couple of places, pressed back by duct tape. There's linoleum on the floor and several unrelated scatter rugs, an old stuffed armchair, a sinking double bed with a voluminous polyester duvet, a set of plywood cupboards above a two-burner electric stove with the choice of ON or OFF. All in all, it's my grandmother's cottage kitchen, and I couldn't be more content.

I moved in in a burst, dragging water from the lake in galvanized buckets, swabbing out the fridge and storing my Whitehorse groceries and a bottle of wine, whacking the rugs against the porch, unloading my clothes into the cupboard with the pots and pans, setting out my stones from the beach at Haines yesterday. Luxury, pure luxury.

MAY 25

I am not so chipper this morning. It's a low, cool day, a clamped-down sky—the reason for damp spirits, I suppose. I live in the mountains, but not every day. From time to time they vanish, buried in cloud. I'm just tired. Leaving home was hectic, people-stuffed, with no time to pause before the next wave. Hectic when I got off the plane, too, figuring out the car, driving straight into the mountains, a winter-bound, formidable landscape only twelve hours from leafy, smelly Toronto. Skagway was depressing and a day among the piles in the tide zone at Haines thrilling. One way or another I've been in a state of constant response. Last night I slept in a clean bed that's my bed, and I slept long, and today is a day without animation, making no demands at all. Full halt.

I sit in my place on the shed stoop where I have spent many hours over the years, getting ready to leave Atlin or arriving in Atlin, reading or writing, looking up blind, my thoughts down some hole, eyeing the slump of Monarch Mountain to the east, cast with snow or free of snow, the ball of willows higher than my cabin hiding the yard, the distance of the yard in one phase or another—bumpy and dry with spent grasses, or gleaming with new, or stiff with snowdrifts. I've been out here on this shallow, peeling step many times, eating a meal, watching the sky, listening to the birds and the sounds of town, the sound of hammering or sawing, the sound of a small plane taking off or landing on pontoons or skis.

Maybe I am exactly in my place in Atlin. The layers of activity I navigate when I am home pare down when I am here. In this place there is physical beauty in endless and serene motion on a scale that rules everything else. Nothing in Atlin is bigger than the mountains or the sky between the mountains or the weather the two of them cook up. I live here in a house the size of a tent, with only enough room for what I need, and only one of what I need— one speed on my stove, one plate, one warm sweater. Time is very long and contains so few items that I have all my choices in front of me and can see all of them at once. There are ten, not a thousand. Maybe fewer than ten.

I suppose, since we moved to cities, there has been too much to respond to. We have more or less abandoned sleep as an alternate realm, stopped remembering what we dreamt in the night, given up reflecting. The ruminative, self-generated occupations of consciousness tend to close down in a busy life. Not everything in our nature is marvellous and worthy of protection, but some things are. There is now too little time to produce the next thought or the next event out of something internal, something in the way of natural inclination or imagination. The dense, speeding field that surrounds us day to day directs what we attend to. We're used to it, but I don't think we're rigged for it. We don't really have the metabolism for it, and some parts of consciousness get lost— sustaining parts of consciousness.

This is my chance here, when I'm a long way from my crammed life and from everybody I'm entwined with. The beauty of the place is the medium, none of it man-made. I can rest and ruminate here, take up the natural activities of consciousness at a pace I can manage.

I SHARE THIS YARD with a fox. Slender and lithe, streaked grey. She just trotted into the yard, not even seeing me till she reached the corner of the shed. When she turns to look at me, her eyes are milky, bleak, as if she has cataracts. Elizabeth is right about who's been throwing dirt around.

MAY 28

Bree, my girl, I loved talking to you on the phone before I left for Atlin. Not because I was about to come here but because it was a family day, all of us assembled at grandfather's and Joon's, all stalwartly in the yard because it's spring and the barbecue had been rolled out of the garage and the plastic taken off the wrought iron, all of us running back inside as often as possible because of a freezing northeast wind. Talking to you topped it off. I'm glad you are in Brooklyn and not Cambodia.

It was the same kind of day as when you and Charlie were home at Easter. Bright and chilly. I have a picture in my mind of the two of you setting off back to New York, that long drive ahead of you in Charlie's old Saab losing reverse gear, you in a slithery Asian skirt, thick sweater and Stetson hat, and Charlie in his button-down shirt, apprehensive. I like Charlie. He's a tall man but has a light touch.

Jesse outdid herself on the salads—noodles shaped like ears, with roasted peppers and saffron, and another one with endive, pear and walnuts. Mark barbecued chicken. Joon baked a salmon and bought two cakes, a chocolate one and a fluffy yellow one like a hat, each with a slab of icing on top, tombstone-like, inscribed with our names, the eight of us who have birthdays this month.

Grandfather picked up Brant mid-morning and drove to Hamilton, his hearing aid in or out, I don't know, to fetch Brant's friend Deborah and her boy Davey. Cathie came, whom I haven't seen in a long time. She is more beautiful now, her hair pure white. She reminded me she is still married to Brant. I said, "But not in your heart?" and she said, "No." Our cousin Mike came with his wife Roz and their two babies. They are training Michala, the girl, not to retaliate when her brother torments her. "Use your words, Michala," they say. I think she should retaliate.

The afternoon went along and we improvised, the way we do. Grandfather drove Jess and the boys to see his tennis club, the big girls got a lift to the subway so they could go to work. Jack, my Jack, practised tennis serves in the road with young Jack. Grandfather saw them from the living room and I asked if his grandson showed any promise. "Too soon to know," he said. Joon tended us, covered the food when it started to dry out, washed the silverware and put it away. "It's a good family," she said. Then you phoned.

I'm here again in Atlin and I was wondering how many times I've been north since the first time in 1990, when you were nineteen and came out to meet me. I worked it out by counting off what you were doing the last ten years. See if I'm right. Montreal for a year after the summer you came out to meet me and we drove home together. You got a place in Westmount and you and Joanna went paint crazy, body-prints on the living-room walls. Then you went to UBC for a year. I have a violet you sent in November, pressed in a card. You stayed on, tree-planting, and met Conor, and I came out to see you a couple of times, sleeping on your floor in Victoria. We took off camping somewhere. Do you remember Denman Island, those mid-Gulf Islands we visited? It was March and rushing spring. The halibut were spawning and we saw eagles all the time picking off their eggs.

I think it was January 1993 when you went to Cambodia to see your dad. Conor followed and you got a job at your dad's little news agency and stayed four years. Leon and I came to see you after the first year. That was a good visit, a long one. I have strong, 3-D memories of our time there, some ache stringing all the pictures together, I don't know why. You and Conor curled asleep on your white bed, blurred under the mosquito net, the cool stone stairs, always in shade, going up to your apartment, your sandals by the door with the thinnest soles, no arch support of any kind, you bargaining over old silk in Khmer in the covered market, me lying on your kitchen floor for the cool of it, resting my eyes, which leaked the whole time, me shopping in the market for anything recognizable to cook, the view from your balcony of the National Palace with its chili-pepper, flutey towers, the orange clouds stacked up at sunset like an explosion, the brown Mekong River sliding past your apartment, walking in the street with you, arm in arm, leaning on your confidence in that overwhelming place, our trip to Angkor Wat, the sad, blackened porches and tunnels, the faint dreaming faces in the walls, the live gum trees bursting through the walls, knuckled roots strangling the rotting stone, the heat and silence.

I went back to see it again, did you know? After you left. I hired a Vespa and driver and went all over the compound, out where the Khmer Rouge have their target practice, where a tourist was shot a week later. I remember the sound at Angkor Wat, the particular whine in the gum trees—some insect—and the high keening sound constant in Phnom Penh, which I thought was the mourning of thousands of murdered Khmer but turned out to be moped tires. I remember the straight-backed old women with silver brush cuts, the Buddhists in marigold robes and parasols, you with your camera, your hair bundled in a scarf (what's the Khmer word?), your brown shoulders a little rounded.

You wrote me one time that soon we'd be in the yard together putting in a garden, but we do not seem to find ourselves in the same yard. Not so far. My yoga friend Kharoon said, if it's what you have, it is for you, but sometimes I wish that it were not this way, that we were a little more in each other's hair. Sometimes I wish we had ordinary times and bickering times and not only our best selves with each other. Do you think we've become a bit enshrined?

Possibly not. I just remembered our blowout on the phone at Christmas. Possibly we are not yet a mother and daughter in porcelain. That's good.

Meantime I'm in Atlin again, my glorious hideout. I'm glad you have your sand dunes and tides on Nantucket when Brooklyn gets too much. I like to think of you digging clams, your hair whipping around. We all need rocking, and nature does it best, don't she.

You are very precious to me. My deep correspondent. Not the writing kind, the other kind, my deep companion.

Much love,
mum

MAY 29

It was snowing when I flipped off Joyce's polyester duvet this morning, and I thought the motorboat ride with Gernot would be scrubbed—which it was, but not because of weather. "Weather would never stop Gernot," Elizabeth said. Gernot is sixty and last year, after training at breakneck speed on the Atlin trails all winter, he skied around Birch Island in a day, a circumference of about a hundred kilometres. Today his boat has motor troubles. I saw him in it, floating on the lake, the engine coughing, when I walked to Elizabeth's.

So Elizabeth and I did one of my favourite hikes instead, loading her two dogs and a couple of foster dogs, the ones who are still up to it, into the back of her old Datsun and driving a few miles out of town to the cemetery. It is unchanged, still the propeller and the wobbly mattress graves I have admired for years. At the south end, high above Pine Creek, we pick up the trail that follows the creek east. It is early spring, the willows barely pricked out in pale green, the shrubs all plum, sap-rising colour, lupines in low purple bundles, bluebells, the first yellow arnica, kinnikinnick in flower, juniper crawling over the ground, clouds breaking up and the sky washed sharp. The air is full of a scent I keep sniffing till I'm dizzy. It's the cottonwoods, their leaves just emerging, sharp like tulips and glossed in some sticky juice, some birthing sap, wild and sweet. What a place.

We walk the rim, the little creek below between its broad gravel borders amiably following the course left to it after all the gold rush mucking around. We come to a gorge where the creek gains volume and noise, spinning in the steep rock walls. Elizabeth yells at the dogs. It's a sheer drop over huge boulders. Once we saw little ducks swirling around in the turbulence as if it were a bathtub, merry in the roar. Somewhere along here is where we spotted a raven's nest two years ago, a great rarity to glimpse anything of the lives of these smart, secretive birds. The nest was a heap of messy sticks suspended over the gorge on an impossible ledge. There would be no practice runs for the young leaving the nest. Do or die. Elizabeth spies the nest again, but there is no family this year.

We stop for lunch farther up, where the trail meets the creek, sitting down in a clutter of driftwood left by the runoff. Elizabeth pulls out the picnic she brought: cheddar, mayonnaise and cream cheese sandwiches, a tomato halved, coffee in a Thermos. I contribute some Swiss chocolate. We chatter and eat, watch the water and the little pines across the way with their brood of yellow cones. Her dog Sumo is very quiet beside us, his nose grabbing and sorting all the smells.

On the return we take the low road, trudging in the gravel along the creek, the sun growing steadier and steadier until by mid-afternoon it fills the sky and loads the air.

I love walks with Elizabeth. She is a keen observer of weather and birds and growing things. She goes out with her dogs every single day, and I believe she is part dog, her observations and intuitions running along dog lines. When I go out with Elizabeth I see better. And she is watching her life, which I like in people too.

I am glad to be a woman for this reason; I can have the conversations I want to have. I can say to another woman, What is it all about, do you think? What have you been able to figure out? How is getting older going for you? A woman will answer with alacrity, as if that is just what she has been mulling over at that moment.

Conversations with men are more oblique. I don't know what men are thinking about. I don't assume they are unreflective or lost down some rabbit hole. I stay curious and hopeful, though it is discouraging when thoughtful men like the writer Jim Harrison say they prefer to talk to women, that women are further along the evolutionary trail than men.

I talk to men all the time in my counselling practice—fathers and husbands, brought to counselling by their kids or their wives. It's my job to try to riddle them.

I assume men live in code, from a woman's point of view. We don't know their lives. Between the sexes, it's anthropological. I know their psychological work is harder. Men have to separate from their mothers, identify separately, whereas women don't have to separate from, only withstand, their mothers. Maybe it takes it out of them. They have to give up that huge, comfortable, gossipy, solicitous circle women spend their lives in. What replaces it for them? What is expected of men now that there are no woolly mammoths left to kill?

IN MY FORTIES I couldn't be around men at all. I was too ratty and lonely. I read Edna O'Brien and lined up with the women in her stories, middle-aged, still lusty women full of longing and humiliation. I had no lover and did not expect to have one ever again, and it rankled like some vestigial spur. I felt abandoned by men. They were done with me, apparently, before I was done with them.

Leon would come home from time to time, looking for friendship, a certain kind of intimacy, and I'd drive him out of my house. Or there would be men in my counselling room, needing so much care and patience, so much bringing along, with their terrible fragility. As soon as they sat down with me I'd pick a fight with them. Why should I be the one to help? How could I? Leon said, don't think of it as gender—but it *was* gender.

Menopause was my time to grind down my life with men, and for a long time I felt I had nothing to say to them, nothing to spare.

I STILL LIVE in the house I moved to ten years ago, when I came back from the Yukon, the property at the top of Algonquin Park. I love my house. It's the best home I've ever had, though if I dropped a match anywhere near it, it would be gone in twenty minutes. It is a dry, old, uninsurable house with several inconveniences. I have no plumbing. Good water runs all over my hill, but I have no well nearby and haul my water by the gallon from further down where there's a well. I fetch it by car in summer when the road is open and by toboggan in winter when the road is full of snow. This has been a pleasant chore so far. I like the effort, strapping the canisters to the toboggan, chugging the half-kilometre up my steep hill. When I'm seventy I will want to drill a well close by.

After I'd been in the house a few years, Leon built me a porch on the north side with a big double-board floor and specially-made screens floor to roof. He salvaged some big frame windows from a sidewalk and every November I lug them out of the back house and fit them over the screens till May, when I take them off again and walk them down the trail. In spring I lay a mattress down on the porch, cover it with a cotton quilt and sleep there most nights till October. I like to see the light change on the porch—the blank spring light across the floor when the trees are bare, the sliding leaf shadows through June and July, the apricot light of August.

Leon has never lived with me again. Well, once he did. After one of his long absences years ago, I asked him to unpack, to stay home for good, and he agreed. I cleared a little room upstairs for his computer gear and he moved in, but it was too late. I had turned into some sort of outlaw, snappish and inconsolable, and wouldn't have him back. After a few months I was ruining us and asked him to leave.

Now, when he's home, he stays down the hill in the first house on the property. In winter, when the trees are bare, I can see his lights. We keep a trail open between our houses and trot back and forth. A few years ago I asked him to set a price on my house, with a few acres around it, and I have it about paid off. I believe this formalizes our separation.

We went to Cambodia together in 1994 to visit Bree. That was the last time we were lovers. Just once, one night or day, in a jet-lag stupor in Bangkok on our way to see her. For the next five weeks we slept side by side on Bree's roof in Phnom Penh, but that half-conscious joining in the hotel in Bangkok was the last slide into our old relation. Before that, it had been a year or two. It takes a long time to unwind from someone. Possibly you never uncouple from someone you really married.

I DON'T SEE MUCH of Leon lately. If he were home, I guess I would. We're neighbours and rely on each other in certain ways. We keep some liveliness between us; we don't let the friendship go. But not too much liveliness. When he's around I'm aware of not stirring things up. I know that if I saw him every day for a week I'd be right back in, hectoring him, telling him everything. The whole band would strike up again, the banjos, zithers, pianos, same as always. The groove of our association is so worn, such a mix of love and exasperation, I would skid into it again.

Nothing has changed. The love never goes. I am out of the habit of Leon, is all.

He said, "I learned a lot from you, Jill. I learned that relationships are hard work and I don't want to do it." But he didn't mean it. He's in another one now. Who wouldn't be, given the chance? I notice that people in their fifties don't turn down love any more than people in their twenties.

WHEN I MOVED to my house ten years ago, I took a job almost right away at a counselling agency in a nearby town. I still work there, three days a week. I didn't mean to find a job so fast. When I came back from the Yukon I had enough money for a while and I wanted to see what would happen if I just waited. But I couldn't stand the freedom. I found it stunningly difficult not to be plugged in anywhere, not to be bound up with people. It was a feeling of being not quite real. If a tree falls in the forest . . . If a woman walks around her house all day unaccountable, is she there?

Leon would phone from somewhere, friends would phone, their voices too far off. A state of mind like sad weather would weigh in. Nothing prompted it, no effort dispelled it. I'd be fine, sitting on my steps in cool autumn light, the last hummingbirds streaking by the house, and contentment would fan out all around me. Then I would stumble, have a troubling dream or lose track of Bree in my heart, or it would seem too thin with Leon and I would see how I maintain the thinness, or I would be lazy with my time. Then I'd be hauled back under a cloud, wake sluggish, find no comfort in myself.

I found out that time on your hands is only precious in relation to the nearness of, the easy access to, its opposite. In those first months after the Yukon, new in my house, no acquaintances or obligations yet taken up, I was a wraith. I had no place anywhere, no footprint, no weight. It was like being caught outside the living world, a ghost at the window.

"WHY DO MEN chase women?" asks Olympia Dukakis in *Moonstruck.* "Because they fear death." That is what I think was the heart of my trouble.

We are the animal with foreknowledge of death. This is the organizing fact in human life, the dilemma that explains everything, I sometimes think. We're smart, but we're going to die. As a hedge we busy ourselves, form attachments, get distracted. We bind ourselves to the earth by a thousand tiny wires, like Gulliver among the Lilliputians, to beat the rap. Why would fame be so attractive, or goods, or reproducing ourselves, or any of our large and small pursuits, if they did not increase the grip we have on the earth? We practise subterfuge, stake ourselves out over as large a surface as possible, because it is incomprehensible that—honestly now—we are going to die.

This is the mental outpost where I lived the first months I was home from the Yukon. I had pulled so many of the lines free, I was snapping in the wind. The time after my summer away was the teeth-rattling part of the trip, not when I was out there, loving my freedom, but later, when I came home and freedom was all I had.

I know I would have accumulated a life if I'd waited it out, if I could have lasted. Fallow ground is pure potential. But I couldn't bear the suspense. I had to jump ship and get a job, sit with families again, talk to people, and let a job solve what I couldn't solve. And it worked. Presto, agitation gone.

JUNE 1

Gradually the days have fleshed out, more and more enjoyable, so that every minute now I look forward to. There are things I do, always the same but in different order—whatever I decide in the moment. Part of the joy is the steady, beautiful weather, the winds calm and the sun riding the sky all day, barely travelling, just easing below the horizon for a few hours after midnight before returning, so every day feels like bounty, like generosity or good fortune, given in boundless portions.

I woke this morning as though I'd been catapulted awake, totally rested, ten hours asleep, with my usual intermission in the cool yard to pee.

Pat said yesterday, on a walk with Elizabeth and Diana and six dogs, that Atlin makes her think of a notion about holy places, everything being in the right balance, all the colours and shapes in perfect relation to each other. It seems possible there is a resonance between spirit and physical or elemental composition, the mountains exactly the right distance from the eye, or from each other, light and water interceding, to set off some kind of perfection, a spiritual sonar that the human solar plexus registers.

My habit is to write in the morning in the shady cabin, stop and eat lunch when the sun is crawling onto the porch, walk for a few hours in the afternoon, plaster myself against the hot porch wall in the evening before I cook dinner. When I'm tired, I pull the curtains and climb into the last square of sunlight in my bed and read till it's gone, till dusk at midnight.

Yesterday I went through the white woods late in the day, slats of sun lighting up the poplars like a clutter of bleached bones. I sat writing in the strawberry field, a clearing that you come upon from the woods like magic, everything swimming together, the line of mountains, trees and sky fluid as current. I stayed a long time, sitting on the ground, whisking ants off my legs, filling my eyes. It was after nine when I sat down in my dazzling cabin to my plate of spaghetti.

I often walk at the south end of town, through the Tlingit village and along the dirt road that comes out at the cemetery with its picket graves. Beyond it are the dogged little pines at the back of the beach where people go for picnics. Sometimes I change my course and leave the road before the cemetery and go over the rocks toward the lake. These rocks are very wonderful—pocked, volcanic, covered in orange lichen and juniper and crackling ground cover from old years. The ground has a dry, shattered look, as if the winter cold had burst the rock, split the ground again and again. Erosion is leaving glittering white skeins of mineral over the orange granite beneath, the way fascia binds human muscle.

JUNE 2

I have a bald eagle on my flagpole. He is eating something, his back to me and to the wind. A seagull has been screeching at him, but he is unperturbed. He was there last night as well, this flagpole being the tallest perch around. I was alerted to his presence by the gulls, miserable and outraged, flying at him. I watched for an hour while he persevered through their onslaught. One or two gulls, once four, flew loops around him, screeching, stretching out their feet at him, warrior-style, never coming closer than a yard. He bore this, feathers upended and dishevelled like a count with a lot to put up with, wary of the gulls, craning his neck at them and cranking open his beak, holding fast. I thought he must be threatening one of their nests—who knows where—but perhaps gulls just hate him on principle, a fellow scavenger.

I like him. He's grumpy and alone.

Now here's something. A raven flies up and, without hesitating a second, lands eye level to the eagle, three feet from him on the pulley. The eagle stops eating. They stare at each other and the raven begins to make a sharp, rocking motion like dry heaves. He is half the size of the eagle but apparently is retching at him. The eagle holds the raven's gaze, maintains his perch, his feathers twiddling in the wind. Now the raven flies off, cackling. The eagle sits immobile and does not eat. When I go to bed he's still there, unkempt, contemplative on the flagpole.

MY MOTHER CLAIMS the sixth decade is the best. "I've tried them all and your fifties are your best," she says.

I prepared for mine with hope. Toward the end of my forties I had the feeling I was approaching an incline, coming to higher ground after a long slog through swamp. I may be describing menopause. At fifty I was pretty well out the other side. My brain seemed to be clearing, the band waves coming in sharper; and without particularly resolving anything, I had stopped hating myself.

I think I managed it by enduring. Gradually I had taken charge of my house—painted enough walls, tunnelled my fingers into the garden dirt enough springs, been the only soul on the hill in enough winter storms, to gain possession. I believe this is how you take hold of yourself, by staying in one place.

When I walk in the mountains in the North, in Atlin or Kluane or in the passes, I sometimes become afraid of bears. When I do, I sit down. I stay where I am, look around until, little by little, I know the place. The birds and small animals I've disturbed resume their activities, my eyes and senses gradually register the ground, the sky, the lay of things. My skin seems to thin. I am breathing rather than thinking, and I have the sensation of being more similar to my surroundings than different, the sensation of being another creature in a certain place. I pass into a different relation to bears, one that I can manage. Then I go on.

Approaching fifty, I was more at home in myself by dint of lasting. Five or seven years after coming back from the Yukon the first time, I had outlasted all the endings I'd been through and had collected, very slowly, a different set of pleasures. Coming up to fifty, I had some ways to replenish myself and please myself, the way being in a little family with Leon and Bree and being a menstruating, moon-bound woman had pleased me.

Coming up to fifty, I knew as sure as anything I was out of trouble, and in a wave of gratitude I decided to throw a birthday party for myself and go on a big outing. The same way I'd done in 1990, I excused myself from work and packed the car for the North. I asked a friend in Toronto if I could use her house, and I invited my family and best friends of twenty years to my birthday. Everybody rallied. They brought photos and told funny memories, made rounds of margaritas in the kitchen, danced on the bare floors—nieces and nephew, Mom and Dad and old friends all mixed together under one roof with me. Everybody but Bree. Bree in Phnom Penh. I made a speech, as if I'd just reached solid ground after a hard swim, as if I were Marilyn Bell hauling out of Lake Ontario. For me the evening had the effect of a rite. I'd waited out the last of something and was now in a light and neutral time, a woman with one chunk of her life over and another starting up.

I BOUGHT A KAYAK the year after the Haida Gwaii trip, and I took it with me when I went to Atlin the summer I was fifty. I bought it without deliberation as a way to continue my experience in Haida Gwaii, a way to be outdoors and travel by water by myself. Unlike my cedar canoe, which takes two to manoeuvre, my kayak weighs only fifty pounds. I can hoist it onto the car roof without help and I can carry it, the combing biting into one shoulder or the other, over portages. My boat is a sea kayak, meant for open water, for the tides and surf of the coasts or the big fresh water of Georgian Bay and the Great Lakes. A sea kayak is an ancient conveyance adapted to waves. The covered deck and narrow cockpit make a seal against water. A paddler can go forth in waves, hunt or travel in the sea, without the boat taking on water and sinking. Kayaks are suited to riled water, but riled water is also their peril. In a sea kayak the danger is waves, waves far from shore during long crossings, waves blowing on cold sea water or on big glacial lakes where there is no shore in reach, where if you capsize you must rescue yourself quickly, get out of the water and back into your boat before you become too cold to move.

I never thought about dumping in the Pacific Ocean in Haida Gwaii, though there was a capsize on that trip. Even paired with the guide, it seems strange now that I did not. I'm amazed when I look at the photographs from the trip and see my life jacket stowed neatly on the deck and remember the currents and waves we blithely navigated, not one of us with a shred of experience. At the time I never thought of drowning.

I do now. When I paddle, except on the calmest days, I always have fear slithering around in me, a dark fish under my heart. I'm afraid of drowning, and for years when I first used my kayak I treated it like a canoe, keeping to smaller lakes where I could see the shore, where wind could never whip up enormous waves. I paddled in Temagami and Algonquin, places that were familiar, gamely lugging my boat over the joins between lakes. I never thought about kayaking in open water; it was enough to have a boat I could handle without a partner. I would go out whenever I liked, paddle, camp, muddle through maps. I would go off-season when there was no one around—in the pale spring when snow was still wadded in the dogwoods along the shore, or late in the year, in November, when the lakes were black and silver and forming ice doilies at the edges.

I like the speed, flashing along with my double blade like a drum majorette, easily outstripping a pair of canoeists. I like the kayak's tidiness, the way it compels order. All baggage is stored below decks, not heaped the way you load a canoe. Bundles must be small as a sleeping bag, or smaller. For a three-day trip I would have eight or ten little parcels, each a different colour, all punched down and waterproofed. Above decks the rules are looser, you can be more idiosyncratic. Some people pay attention to aerodynamics and keep a sleek look on deck. Some don't and stash all sorts of paraphernalia under the shock cords: billies, rain gear, fishing tackle, cameras. Even pruned to the minimum, a chilling assortment of equipment is strapped on deck as mere safe practice: pump, throw bag, sponsons (oblong air bags that can be inflated in foul weather or in a capsize to stabilize the boat), sea anchor, map, compass, spare paddle. Once the kayak is outfitted, kayakers get themselves arrayed head to foot: neoprene bathing cap, wetsuit, paddling jacket, spray skirt, booties, suction-pad gloves. Since all the big water in this country is ice-cold, kayakers are always rigged to fight death. This gives a sobriety, a formality to kayak expeditions that I both enjoy and resist, comparing it to the way, in a canoe, you put on your running shoes and jump in.

FOR YEARS I loved my kayak without exploring its main purpose—big water. A few summers ago I ventured onto Georgian Bay, a natural home for a sea kayak, with unbounded water and a wonderful ecology, and once I started going out there, I had to learn some technique. Georgian Bay has jump-up weather and myriad look-alike islands. When I'm on the bay, I am problem solving all the time; this is the joy of it. Of the problems to be solved "Where am I?" looms large. I am not so proficient a map-reader that I always know. I have a good memory for landscape, though, and I use visual handholds carefully. Through the trip, besides paddling, I spend a fair amount of time estimating where on earth I am, proving myself right, or close to right, or dead wrong, paddling around lost for two hours. This is exciting.

A change in the weather on Georgian Bay is probable, even within a single day. The wind shifts, waves come up or slack off, from one hour to the next, and this brings the occasion to change my stroke or tack, choose where I'll go and what I'll put up with.

Balancing my ever-nervous state is exhilaration. Water and sky wheel, and I am completely taken up contending with them.

Georgian Bay is a marvellous place, even under hard use. Offshore is a heavy necklace of bony pink islands, the rock fissured and whirling, great laps of smooth rock gliding into the water. Pine, juniper and cedar grow on the larger islands, the pine taking wind-bent, Group of Seven shapes. Poison ivy twines through the rock cracks, the last of the massasauga rattlers snooze out of sight, spiders set up their webs and egg sacs overnight. In summer the islands feel tropical, virtually treeless, baking in the sun. Waves boom on the shoals further out, and the air carries a scent like flowers.

WHEN I TOOK my boat to the Yukon in 1995, I didn't know the high-lights of sea kayaking. I had been fooling around on canoe routes in Temagami. Over the summer I dipped into some of the smaller lakes around Atlin, stroking along the bright water, duck-hounding, float-ing under the mountains, never staying out overnight. Atlin Lake was too rough for small boats that year, whitecaps scuffing up every day, the wind rushing off Llewellyn Glacier in the south. The times I put my boat out, I stayed close to shore.

I was unreconciled to being timid. I had a constant sense of nib-bling the edges of the venture I really wanted to make. I would imagine crossing the distance to Atlin Mountain, some five miles away, seeing it rise above me, drawing into its atmosphere. I thought about travelling through Torres Channel, paddling among the moun-tains, leaving the town behind, and I began to long for the nerve.

I believe this has to do with starting late. If I were a young woman, even a young woman afraid of drowning, I could take my time. I could paddle in Temagami and Algonquin, roll out of my boat into warm water, play in the little surf on Lake Nipissing beside the summer swimmers, brace in the easy waves. I could swim with my boat for years and it would be an easy move to colder water, to big-ger wind and waves, to travelling with a load, to travelling in fog and in darkness.

As it is, I have no time to wait. I have to go afraid or not go. Being out of doors—anywhere outdoors that has no buildings and bears no sign of our foolishness—is the best solace I'll ever have. Therefore, on the return drive from Atlin that year, I stopped at Lake Superior, wriggled into my wetsuit in a hedge and put my boat on Old Woman Bay. The day was calm, but Lake Superior is an inland sea; it breathes. Following the face of the bay, my boat rising and falling on the swells along the rock wall, I felt like a mote sliding over enormous liquid lungs, allowed there on sufferance by some colossus. Paddling out of the gentle coves over the next few days gave me no better sense of acquaintanceship. The beauty of the lake, the looming cliffs and scarps of stone, the purity of the water, the folds of rock plain beneath me even in thirty feet of water, only added to the fearsomeness of the lake. Better an opaque surface than this spangled open vault over the side of my boat.

I came back successive years, sampling the shoreline, thrilled. I am afraid, probably more afraid than most people stirring around these places, but I am also euphoric, snapped alive. I love my chipper boat, I love where it can go and everything that happens when I go.

Jack sometimes paddles with me now. I go alone or I go with Jack. Jack has been paddling since he was a boy, and while I was nudging around Superior's shore Jack was paddling alone to the Slate Islands, twelve kilometres straight out in a dense fog.

Jack is my lonely twin. I've known him for years, since the first year I moved to my place in Powassan. We were both in a drawing group I used to go to in North Bay. I noticed him when he was telling a story, waving his arms around. He has nice arms, the skin smooth, the veins close to the surface, worming over the muscle. Jack has veins in his arms that nurses in a blood donor clinic would dream about. His story was about being camped somewhere and leaving the tent flap open and the tent blowing down in a storm that came up in the night. His manner conveyed that he is a person who doesn't have to make a point of his experience.

When I go with Jack I can get into the places I want to go, but I still have to get out on my own.

JUNE 3

Spring comes on in Atlin minute by minute. The buckbrush back of the playing field is out in lime green raindrops. Every view is pale green and purple. My hedge daintily fills in. The cotton-woods are sprouting pointy buds, their smell musky and sweet, wafting like a mist. The weather is stunning. My hand laundry drying on the fence gets the colour knocked out of it by a huge blank sun. The whole town looks bleached. It takes till nine o'clock at night for a little blue to creep in.

I walked along the road out of town this afternoon to a turnoff that climbs Como Mountain, the road gradually showing long views down the lake, the day shimmering, the sun illuminating water in the air, the sides of the mountains like plum velvet. There is a house for sale at the crest, a plain house set back on a dirt driveway, the yard cut out of the bush and cluttered with projects—a pile of old windows, a pyramid of stovewood, loosely stacked, a mound of shingles under a disintegrating tarp, some rough-cut buildings, an animal pen empty of animals. The owner saw me looking and waved me in, a stout, middle-aged man in a worn flannel shirt, his face shiny red.

227

"I'm not expecting to buy a house. I just saw your sign."

"May as well come in anyway. I'll show you around."

He's from Kapuskasing, a francophone. He told me the same story I've heard over and over in Atlin. He and his wife came here on holiday, bought property on the spot and moved here when he retired, full of plans. He's done a lot of them, they're around him like a brood: a greenhouse, a vegetable garden with brought-in soil, fences, an ex-pigpen, a workshop and guest house—the doors still to be put on, glass to be set in the windows—a tree house for the grandkids. The place looks like all the horses were let out of the starting gate at the same time and everybody's just into the third quarter.

"Have a look at the main house. I'm putting in a shower. About got it hooked up to the hot water tank."

It was a wonderful house, the kitchen chartreuse and turquoise in real Quebec style, the living room a crush of family photographs, crocheted afghans, trays of seedlings ready to plant. The porch by itself was worth the selling price, an open, plank floor with an old bench car seat suspended from the roof by heavy chains and the best Atlin view I've ever seen, a pure south swoop all the way to Llewellyn Glacier, shining like a pearl.

"The only thing is, my wife wants to move. Now I've got this high blood pressure, she wants to be closer to a hospital. She's got a sister in Owen Sound. We might try there."

"My god. How long have you been here?"

"Seven years."

JUNE 5

Home starts to loom, like walking toward a crowd on a lawn, the people taking shape and recognizable. How do we live with so many confreres, so many lives we're following and woven into? I never solve this. I need to be entwined and I need to be unentwined. I have been wolfing down this time alone in Atlin.

Too steep an arc, this trip. I was barely here, barely sprawling, brain released, before the countdown started. Five more days. Now it's three. Going home has uprooted my sleep. I woke in the twilight this morning and it took a while to fall back. I thought of my niece's dance recital, Jack setting off to Superior, a twelve-year-old I'm seeing at work. I begin to take it all up again even here.

Yesterday I walked up Monarch Mountain. The weather was about to change. I left at four in white afternoon, in an unbroken outpour of sun, but soon there was a haze over the sky and a circle round the sun. Little by little the sky furred up. The sun was barely a burr by the time I came down.

I never plan to climb Monarch Mountain. I don't set it as a goal. It's just that, once underway, it's hard to stop. The climb has its own momentum.

My body always wants to stop immediately. It is a short climb, Atlin's local climbable mountain, but a steep one. Unless you're a goat, you will stop, out of breath, often. All the way through the climb, however high I go, my body wants to stop. My lungs want to, my knees want to, but my senses never do. They are always lighthearted and always prevail. This time I had no snacks along and only half a litre of water. My stomach growled all the way, but climbing is wonderful, the perspective changing foot by foot. The lake and islands, flattened against each other at ground level, tip out and come into view as I climb. The islands in front of Atlin Mountain, the long lap at its base, the scattering of islands along the coast of Birch, Torres Channel, the current visible—all these details that are normally pressed flat, that I don't know about from town, come into being.

As I climb, the season falls back. Anemones have had their time at ground level but are blooming, exquisitely fresh, higher up.

I pass arnica at its peak, the scent of budding poplars floats around again, there are flowers not seen at all at lower heights—mountain avens trembling on their stalks. It is spring, the variety wonderful and amazing, everything tumbling to life in this long-light place, succulents and ground covers, tiny, wind-outfoxing flowers.

Gradually I leave the realm of air, the looking-out, held-in-the-air sensation, and enter the realm of the mountain, drawn into the mountain, an atmospheric change. A sea change. The mountain presents itself. I am in its breath, enfolded in a rare and dense environment, elemental ground, smelling of rock and earth. As I climb higher and higher, I come more and more to earth. The hidden mountain absorbs me.

On Monarch it is a calm day and I would have liked to go on. I have the spirit for it. I am cautious, though, about being hungry, and about my knees. At a certain point I turn around.

My feet are aching and fed up by the time I get down. I am glad for the loan of Tony's bike to get back to town, in spite of its inhuman seat.

JUNE 9

I get up at five, as I have many times when I'm taking the mail truck to Whitehorse to catch the plane. I slept in my sleeping bag so I could leave Joyce with clean linen. I make tea, black because I gave the milk to Elizabeth last night. I rinse the cup, throw the last of the water out the door, close my duffle and backpack, and drag them to the gate. There's no sight of Atlin Mountain this morning, cloud bundled on the lake. The neighbour has the key. I push the lock on the door and pull it closed, and stand in the road, listening to the sparrows frisking in the hedge in the grey morning. Pretty soon I see the driver's lights coming along the road. Colin didn't forget.

Now comes the part that always feels low and frayed. I am neither here nor there. The mail truck takes the well-known road. I'm the only passenger. If I close my eyes for a while and open them, I still know exactly where we are. We come to Minto Mountain, squatting like a pyramid on the lake. We cross into Yukon Territory and I glance west to see the survey line. I do these things by rote. White Mountain on the right. I recognize the tower I climbed to the year before last. There was still six feet of snow on top, dripping off an eaten drift.

I never leave casually. I never doze on this drive. It's not that I think I won't be back; I trust by now I will. And probably it won't have changed much when I come. Probably the same dusty mail truck, the same three runs a week. It's that it's always such a time. When I come to Atlin I am temporarily at large. I swing by a rope outside my own life. I look in the windows, see how everything is going, swing free of it.

At the airport there's time to sit outside. I can hear the passenger call from out here. Sun is breaking up the high cloud. It might be a beautiful day in the Yukon. Maybe I will see Atlin when we fly over in an hour, tiny geometry in a huge white rumple of mountains.

This is a nice flight, either way. It has a small-towny feel. You can guess who everybody is: teachers coming back from holiday, mothers with children going to visit relatives in the south, businessmen from Calgary or Vancouver. Passengers talk to one another as though this were the local bus. I sit next to a lawyer, plying through a court transcript. We pass too far inland to see Atlin.

In Vancouver airport the pace picks up, and I am less moony. There are electronic problems, the computers won't issue boarding passes, and the staff cope heroically in an airless waiting room, a planeload of Asian passengers fanning themselves patiently. I fall into a reverse prejudice in this company. What handsome people they are—slender, glossy-haired, smooth-faced. We Caucasians must look like a bunch of clacking chickens. Several impossibly young women are lugging fat, sleeping babies in their arms, two of whom, when we finally get on board, have seats in the row beside me. For five hours there isn't a peep out of these babies, their mothers completely devoted to making them comfortable, anticipating their every need. I don't see a single magazine flip open or headset go on, not a single lapse in vigilance. I want to be a Chinese baby. In Toronto airport I see them greeted by ecstatic grandparents, the babies awake, refreshed, laughing at midnight.

Outside I smell Toronto—the thick, moist, oxygeny air that broad-leafed trees exude—and feel darkness, strange and consoling, like being sent to bed at last. I get into the leather back seat of a limo and give directions to the silent driver, and in half an hour I am in bed, upstairs in my parents' house, the house I grew up in, watching the leaves rock in the street lamp, listening to their whispering, slithery sound.

I WENT WEST in my car in 1990 like a person burned down, but I came back with seeds in my pocket for the rest of my life. To go into these last places, to go alone or to go with the companion I have found, long after I was content to have no companion, is all I'll ever need.

Eleven

SUPERIOR

J ack asked me to go on a kayaking trip to Lake Superior the second winter we were lovers. I mulled it over all spring. The trip would be in late September, when any clemency in the weather would be over, October storms coming on. Our destination, the Slate Islands, is protected parkland, twelve kilometres out from Terrace Bay on the north shore of Lake Superior. Jack had been there in 1995, three springs before. He told me about a beautiful group of islands, steep and densely wooded, with huge, wild beaches facing pure horizon on the south side. He had seen caribou swimming between the islands. We would go with another couple: Graham, a friend of Jack's, a good paddler and trained guide, and his wife Adrienne, a writer. Graham and Adrienne would take a tandem; Jack and I would paddle our own boats.

I wanted to go and I was afraid to go. I dithered silently for months, and every time I concluded it was beyond me and gave my answer to Jack, he seemed not to take it in, until at last we were sitting over dinner with Graham and Adrienne one night in August drawing up a list of who'd bring what.

I liked them, a young, versatile couple, long together, but I didn't know them, and Jack and I had never spent more than a few days together at a time, nor were we much in each other's confidence at the time. I don't think he had any idea how apprehensive I was, how miserably I had been imagining trying to land on a beach in surf, or continuing to paddle if there was no beach to land on, or how to manage any of the things I had never done in my life in autumn on the biggest lake in the world. One night in bed, when going on the trip finally seemed inevitable, I told him glumly, "Jack, if I get in trouble out there, I hope you'll help me."

IT WAS FALL on Lake Superior, the hills dusky garnet. We camped the first night on Agawa Bay in a public campground with hot showers and transport trucks roaring by on Highway 17, setting up in the sand back of the beach, cooking pea soup in the dark, thoroughly excited. We'd driven all day in tandem, Graham and Adrienne ahead of us, their Toyota looking like a blocky keel under their big two-seater kayak. By the second night we made it to Neys Provincial Park, shut down for the season, deserted except for a maintenance crew cleaning up. Neys is a ravishing place a few hours past Wawa, established as a park because of a geological phenomenon at one end of a long driftwood beach: the scarred taproot of an ancient volcano, eroded and worked over the last ten thousand years by crashing waves. One of the staff gave us leave to park for a dollar a night and launch from the beach. We strolled through the scrub onto the beach and there were the Slates, faintly visible on the horizon, a gauzy hump to the southwest.

There was too much wind to launch the next day. Stately breakers rolled in, spray flying off their backs, the sun buried in glinting, gunmetal clouds. We packed a picnic and marched down the beach in rain gear and hiking boots. I wore my Swiss Army cape, a rubberized canvas affair down to my ankles, completely waterproof, though incapacitating. Huge rock sculptures hunched at the waterline, Henry Moore bronzes, scoured to satin by tiny grains of sand spinning in the waves. We spent all afternoon clumping over the rocks, Jack yelling with delight when the waves burst on the point, sprawling water over the rocks, shedding it into the lake to be hauled up again.

Nor had the wind dropped the second morning. I would gladly have stayed on the beach again, but Graham, accustomed to getting the better of physical situations, urged that we move on and look for another angle of approach. We packed up in a waft of warm air, the lake still blowing summer off its face while the land cooled.

Terrace Bay is a pulp and paper town on the north shore, the shortest point between the mainland and the Slates. When we got

there it began to rain and the wind cut off, the lake still rolling
and huffing but setting up no whitecaps. The islands were suddenly
very close. We went down to the beach to look. It was drizzling
and glum, but there was a channel of smooth water past the surf
zone, safe access onto the lake. We had a chance.

I knew I'd be the one to say the word, and I said, "Well, let's
go." The men whooped and we went into motion like things that
have been drifting at random and suddenly coalesce and find their
purpose. This crossing is what we came to do. We took the boats
off the roofs and down to the shore, pried the hatch covers off,
wadded bundle after bundle below decks. We moved the cars away
and locked up, took to the bushes to worm into our wetsuits and
clammy paraphernalia, traded off final impossible items to whoever
had a pocket of room. Jack took my frying pan and billy, strapped
the covers on his hatches, rammed his hat on his head and eased
the tail of his boat into the water. I was already floating, my hands
trembling on my paddle. We made our way out past the surf zone
and the bottom fell away.

The lake was in a state of queasy, lolling swells; some monstrous thing, temporarily dozing off. I put my rudder down,
yanked my hat and gloves off, got Jack on my right side, thirty feet
away. I would have liked to tie myself to him, but it wouldn't have
helped. I couldn't rest, not trusting the slack, wanting to drag the
islands closer. I paddled the twelve kilometres without a break,

Jack rising and falling serenely beside me on ten-foot swells, Graham and Adrienne on our other side, keeping company. After a while I was warding off seasickness and needed to keep my paddle in the water to brace and ground.

The wind held off. We got into a gap between the islands and the big waves stopped. We paddled into a bay in late sun, and it was like coming into a Haida camp a hundred years ago, the water crystal and still, the steep beach sickle-shaped, caked in rolling pebbles, the trees backlit, laying shade into the water.

We landed, and jumped for joy. We'd left the world and come here on our own power, and we were all alone. Even the birds had gone.

IT DOES REMIND ME of Haida Gwaii—the pure water, cobble beaches, collapsing wild woods. Here it's spruce trees, thin and toppling, wrapped in crinkled green lichen. The ground is thick with autumn rot and windfall, a million shooting spores, wet-scented fungus and mushrooms, caribou trails.

We hiked today, explored the body of our island, taking the caribou labyrinth in an arc that brought us down again to the shore, following a maze of trails the animals have made, elegant and steady, the easiest, most logical route over the island. The forest is hectic and magical, the spruce trees pressing on one another, the individual trees fragile, their lower branches thin and brittle, reaching straight out and frequently snapped off. Jack thinks they are being devoured by the lichen covering them. In a coastal way, the fallen ones nurse other growth, a wild rumple of mosses and lichens of every kind. There are thousands of mushrooms, frail ones with filament stalks and tiny, brilliant knobs, huge saffron umbrellas on top of milky stems. These plants are pure sex; minute, unabashed genitals, a slippery, showy fusion of male and female that's part thrusting and part rilled and round.

We follow a path that takes us up to the crest of the island, to a southern view of the near islands and out over an empty, aluminum surface as far as the eye can see. We go down again to the shore and walk back along peach-coloured slate that is turned on edge like a worn deck of cards, softened and smoothed where the waterline has worked it away.

After lunch the others go paddling and I walk down the beach. The hills rise steep, aspen-covered, the trees turning amber, dark spires of spruce shooting through the gold. Along the waterline the dark rock is splashed with orange lichen. Mountain ash are in berry along the shore. Paddling in yesterday to the camp that Jack remembered, we passed many beaches, always stone, some so fine and smooth we could drag the kayaks up on them, some pale and jagged, some cobble. Each of them has a huge throw of driftwood high above the waterline, the print of winter storms.

THE WIND is in the east the next morning, an opportunity to visit the rugged south side. We are tucked in our boats before the rain starts, a fine, out-of-the-way drizzle. We paddle round the west point, and after a while there is nothing to my right but horizon and on the left, huge beaches, a succession of ragged coves, sheer and tremendous, grottoes draped in ferns, mad sculptures shaped by waves, juts of rock set on edge straight as ships. Between two massive capes of rock, boulders the size of cars are jammed, flung there who knows when. Farther on, a wall of rock has shattered but holds intact, keeping its cracked form like a windshield in a wreck. We paddle from one fabulous view to the next, like tourists with the wonders of the world lined up for us. We land in an enormous curve of tiny pebbles and eat in thin rain on six feet of dry beach under a leaning shelf of rock. Graham hands out soup, and we are grinning. We feel like castaways. This is all we hoped for, the best it could be.

After lunch I do not want to go on to the lighthouse at the halfway point and decide to start back. I have a constant sense of pushing my luck in this extreme place. Jack accompanies me and we go slowly, trailing into the shallow coves we passed this morning. One has a floor like crusted jewels, rose and turquoise stone in crystal water, the dark walls cupping over our heads.

The rain strengthens and a headwind comes on. We paddle side by side, resting behind an island before the last leg. We see

Graham and Adrienne coming along in their tandem, the only moving shapes in a dim grey ball of water and sky.

Jack cooks one of his peculiar meals tonight. Lentil stew, lurid in the light of the kerosene lamp, potatoes baked in the fire and a can of sardines, placed on a log out beyond the tarp, all topped off with dried fruit soaked in hot rum.

I LIKE TO TENT with Jack, his parcels all laid out by mine, the nice order of him, the two of us pressed in together but self-contained. His clothes never ball up with mine, he doesn't disturb anything I have laid down or elbow me accidentally. I like being with a person deft at being alone and glad to be with me.

"This is the first time we've spent more than three days together, Jack."

"Is it? How do you like it?"

"I like it."

I contrast us with Graham and Adrienne, the difference in the couples—the old young couple and the new old couple. In temper we seem reversed. Graham and Adrienne are partners since high school, easy together, everything for them still ahead, how it all will go. The line between them rides loose with the sense of plenty of time. Jack and I have so much already behind us, already gone as a possibility. We are ardent and careful. I could almost count the time we have, if I could just see it, before the next rogue wave. I feel as though Jack and I met between calamities. Sometimes I send up a little plea—I don't know to what, to the maple trees—for a long intermission. I don't think that's crazy. What do old new lovers have for each other? The death of their parents. Their own decline. Humour, if they're lucky. Thankfulness. Skill. Not so bad, perhaps.

242

WE MEANT TO LEAVE yesterday but put it off because of a fine south wind, perfect wind to paddle to the south side again and perfect wind, if it had held, to push us back to Terrace Bay. We don't know what the weather has in store: the radio batteries gave out.

In the event, the wind changed. We had our splendid day yesterday and glided down our island early this morning prepared to make the crossing. When we left the lee, the north wind broke on us so forcefully we could barely make headway. Paddling as hard as we could, we tacked east to another island and landed behind it. Nothing to do but wait out the wind.

The next day was the first day of October, the month of storms, and we get as far as the sandbar we landed on days ago, the two-sided beach Graham calls a tombola, bounded on one end by a high bloom of land, and joined at the other to the main part of the island. We have now moved to the farthest edge of shelter. There's nowhere to go but across Jackfish Channel to the mainland.

We wait differently. Adrienne and I are content. After a morning of slashing rain, the weather clears and we move around our narrow turf in bright wind, keeping a little fire going, making teas and soup, the two of us assenting to the temper of the lake. Graham paces, watches the wind rough the water, thinks how to get us out. Jack spans the difference, temperamentally more ready to wait than Graham but sympathetic to the task of getting home. The two stand bundled against the wind, conferring.

We are probably not in mortal danger. If we try the crossing, the waves, so far, are not big enough to capsize us, but we are at risk of wearing out against the wind and being forced far off course. We have no radio contact, no forecast, no chance of passersby, a limit to our food.

Jack and I take a walk in the afternoon along the trails to the south, with high views of the coast and spongy breaks in the trees, where we crouch and watch the wind tear at the water. Wind rocks the woods, the little spruces gyrating on their roots, lifting the thick moss around them. How does anything hold in this place? Without the trails it would be impossible to move. The undergrowth is a tangle of windfall, young spruce and fir, outrageous fungi, chines and crevassed rock with deep moss throats, lathered birch, aspen, broken spruce drizzling pale lichen—a fragile tumult.

Graham joins us and we stop at an east view to take our bearings, the men ankle-deep in verdant moss, murmuring and plotting.

I sit above a crevice, watching the sunlight flicker in the trees.

Possibly this is gender, the men preoccupied with getting out, the women musing and acquiescent. Or perhaps it isn't. Graham is a guide, in the habit of moving people. Jack can go either way. Sometimes he stays and waits, sometimes he travels. He wanted to try for it this morning, before the rain broke. He thought there was time.

Or maybe the situation itself creates what we have. We are wind-bound. On this lake it is inevitable. Some restlessly problem-solve and some poke the fire and wait, forward motion in balance with holding motion, till something shifts. Adrienne lies on her Therm-a-Rest, reading. I leave the men and follow the caribou paths, letting the animal lead. Going along, climbing and bending, I seem to anticipate their nature by these perfect paths. The hollows the caribou make are the right size for humans; the way they choose is always the least arduous, the most graceful. A branch snags my hat. I puncture my nose on a twig and dab it with sphagnum moss. I go into that slight feeling of fusion, boundarylessness, I have in certain places. My hands and feet seem to become large, more pliant. This time I am linked to a shy, soft-walking animal. I climb a steep hill, and when I can look up, two caribou are in front of me, their big dark rumps to me, their necks strained around, their eyes rolled to see me. Then they buck and crash off through the trees. I find a shed antler on the ground, a gliding shape, mahogany-coloured.

•

IN THE END we spend two nights on the beach, slowly draining ourselves making plans to leave and trying to leave. A strange predicament, strangely tiring: the place that enchanted us is unquittable.

On the third morning we get up before light, eat a cold breakfast, and send Graham and Jack off in the tandem to Terrace Bay—or whatever shore they can make—to get rescue for Adrienne and me. The wind screams on, but the balance between going and waiting has tilted; they will go. Adrienne and I climb the north cliff by separate paths to watch them. It is my Haida tableau: the women on shore with the force of their thoughts, the men in the boats. When I'm high enough I see the kayak, a battling little needle setting a good angle, making good time, a red and a yellow dot paddling.

When they are out of sight I climb down to the beach and take down my tent. If we are here tonight, I'll tent with Adrienne. We squat by the fire, find our companionship. After a while she goes to nap and I settle myself in a pile of logs on the west side. Little by little the day warms. I shed my parka, fleece pants, hat. The wind drops. A couple more hours' wait and we all could have paddled out together.

Early in the afternoon a wide motorboat comes into the bay like the arrival of modern times. An easygoing man from town drives the boat, Jack and Graham with him. They made Terrace Bay by strength and found Earl in his house, having coffee. At first he declined to make the trip, but after a while he saw the flag outside sagging and agreed to make a run.

I do not like to leave this way—by Caesarean section—but that is how we leave. I stand braced in the boat, facing backwards, the islands growing hazy, getting away, the caribou walking on their trails.

When we reach shore it's all motion again—unloading the kayaks, hitching Earl's boat to the trailer, drawing it out of the water, saying our thanks, finding car keys and packing up. We make a late lunch on the hood of the truck—instant hummus and pita—and stand talking in a rush. No matter how good a trip has been, there's always some mix of relief, some caving in, at the end. When a trip is over, some part of me is relieved to dash into a Quik-Mart and buy nachos. For a while anyway, I'm glad to come in from so much vitality.

Jack pre-empts a plan to drive as far as Wawa for the night and turns in at Pukaskwa, a bulge of land where the highway leaves the coast, a national park, unmaintained but open this time of year. He's about done in and chooses a site abruptly, throws up the tent while I fetch water from the lake and start a makeshift meal. Graham and Adrienne find us and we eat in a pale circle of light from our candle lanterns. We say our goodbyes. Graham has to work the day after tomorrow and they'll need an early start.

HEAVY FROST in the morning, the fly stiff and the bushes silver-white. My bags are too rigid to stuff. We get underway and gradually reach the hardwoods in Superior Park, their colour further along now, deeper into fall. We slow on the big hills, crane for views of the lake. We're coming down now, leaving Superior, a geographical and emotional plunge. In Blind River, at the end of the day, I negotiate a big motel room. We each have a bed, with the same Van Gogh print over the headboards. We take weary and grateful baths, and walk around town before finding a place to eat. Being indoors is like being stuffed in a closet, but we're too tired to care.

In the morning Jack checks the oil in the truck and tightens the kayak ropes. We walk in glistening frost to a donut shop for coffee and bagels to go. It's a good drive all day. I read *Tales of the Great Lakes* to Jack and we imagine trips we could take. Jack drives me home. Rounding the last climb in the road, I see my house, tall and quiet, through the trees, the board and batten starting to grey, the maples pure yellow, pressing in. Seeing them reminds me it's an anniversary. Eight years here, almost to the day.

Jack parks behind my old 4Runner and helps me unload. I unlock the door and the big square room greets me, pale and cool, everything as I left it. I make tea and we drink it on the porch in two armchairs. It was a good time. It's good to sit here, too.

When Jack goes I stay on the porch, the silence slowly coming in. The trees are at their peak. Even the air is stained yellow. A few leaves start to drift down. I expect an early fall.

ACKNOWLEDGEMENTS

IN GETTING GOING on this book I am grateful to Jan Walter for early encouragement and for the suggestion that I bring a person into the description of landscape.

Love and thanks to Marni Jackson, who has egged so many of us on, a wonderful writer and friend.

Thanks near the end of the writing to Anne McKenzie for lavish feedback and good suggestions, every one of which I took.

I'm very lucky to have landed at Random House. All my thanks to Anne Collins and Susan Roxborough and every person in the place for their kindness and help at every turn and for making this a so much better book.

I am especially grateful to Leon and to Bree, my most important readers, for their generosity in letting me tell my version.

My mother and father taught all four of us to love words and to find comfort in writing. Their influence is the slow-acting wave, the one that started long ago and has been gathering all my life. They still set the standard in every way I can think of.